12 Steps fo[...]
Life-Changing[...]

Success is not a destination. Rather, it is a journey; a way of life. That applies directly to what we're trying to do through this book. We're not trying to reach some destination, perfection, or spiritual maturity, or whatever you want to call it. We're trying to change the way we make our journey through this life, making sure we do our best to live each day.

On any trip into unfamiliar territory, it's easy to take a wrong turn and get lost for awhile. Taking wrong road doesn't mean you've blown your entire trip; just that you're going to be inconvenienced for a few minutes.

We all goof once in a while and do something we know we shouldn't do, or say something we shouldn't say. We all take wrong turns now and again, and the only thing to do when that happens is to turn around and get back on the right road.

Take the first step. It's never too late.

Robert A Schuller

Also in
Orient Paperbacks

Positive Imaging
Power of the Plus Factor
Why Some Positive Thinkers Get Powerful Results
Treasury of Courage and Confidence
Achieve Success and Happiness
Living with a Purpose
Success is Never Ending, Failure is Never Final!
Tough Times Never Last, But Tough People Do!
Practical Ways to a Powerful Personality
Secrets of Success
Success in 30 Days
10 Steps to Positive Living

12 Steps for Life-Changing Power

Dump Your Hang-ups

Without Dumping Them on Others

Orient Paperbacks

DELHI | MUMBAI | HYDERABAD

To

John and Donna Crean

whose vision and generosity made possible the restoration and renewal ministry of Rancho Capistrano. It was for such a purpose that they donated Rancho Capistrano, and now thousands of people are being aided in their spiritual growth. Because of their vision, the place has become a centre to inform and inspire individuals in their recovery process.

So I dedicate this book to them as an expression of thanks and love.

www.orientpaperbacks.com

ISBN 81-222-0324-8

1st Published in Orient Paperbacks 2003
3rd Printing 2005

Dump Your Hang-ups Without Dumping Them on Others

Cover design by Vision Studio

Published in arrangement with
Fleming H. Revell, U.S.A.

Published by
Orient Paperbacks
(A division of Vision Books Pvt. Ltd.)
Madarsa Road, Kashmere Gate, Delhi-110 006

Printed in India at
Jay Kay Offset Printers, Delhi-110 041

Cover Printed at
Ravindra Printing Press, Delhi-110 006

Contents

Foreword by Dr. Robert H. Schuller

1. The Power of Recognising Your Powerlessness ... 11

The Twelve Steps Are for You

The Power of Powerlessness

2. God Will Restore You ... 26

Needed: An Understanding of God's Love and Care

It's Never Too Late

How to Obtain Faith

3. Turn Your Life Over to God ... 45

Are You Still Fighting?

Always Remember: Father Knows Best

You've Got to Push the Button

Surrender Is a Constant Process

Guilt

Afraid to Trust Feelings

Trying to Learn the Rules
Not Trusting Others
Rigidity

4. **Through the Magnifying Glass** ... 65
Three of the Most Dangerous Shadows
Unawareness
Resentment
Fear
The Apostle Who Saw Himself
Your Personal Inventory

5. **The Importance of Confession** ... 89
Confession Brings Release
Who Will Hear My Confession?
Confessing When You Haven't Done Anything Wrong
The Confession Session

6. **Getting Ready to Deal with the Ghosts That Haunt You** ... 105
Four Things to Remember
Be Patient
Stay Positive
Communicate with God
Be Aware of Your Feelings
Scripture Will Encourage You

7. **Okay, Lord, It's All Yours!** ... 117
Accomplishing Great Things
A Common Denominator: Humility
One at a Time

It's Okay to Feel Bad
If You Can't Eliminate It, Use It

8. Getting Ready to Say "I'm Sorry" ... 132
Make a List and Check It Twice
Beginning with the Ones You Love
Is Restitution Necessary?

9. Time to Make Amends ... 139
It's Hard to Say "I'm Sorry"
Something We Should Have Learned in Kindergarten
What One Man Can Do
The Importance of the Horizontal
The Ghosts of Unresolved Guilt
A Time to Keep Things to Yourself
An Apology Isn't Enough
The Danger of Losing Ground

10. Keeping Your House in Order ... 166
Regular Maintenance
Don't Stop Now!
Periodic Spot Checks
Write It Down

11. Get Closer to God ... 179
Prayer
Practising Meditation
Reading the Bible
The Importance of Fellowship
Moving Through the Day

12. **Spread the News** ... 195

The Importance of the Foundation

God Is Blessing You Now

I Was Blind, But Now...

Are You Ready to Live?

The Journey Begins

Endnotes

Foreword

All around us millions of people are living in bondage. They are held captive by addictions to drugs, alcohol, sex, and work. Their lives may be bent and twisted by events and circumstances of long ago. They long for freedom, but they don't know how to get free.

Perhaps *you* are one of these people.

If you are struggling to gain your freedom, or if you know someone who is caught up in such a struggle (and who doesn't?), then please keep reading, because this book is going to take you on a very important journey: a journey that can help you learn how to make a dramatic change in your life.

It is a special pleasure for me to be able to write the foreword to this book because I know the help and healing that can be found within its pages. There is wisdom here, wisdom combined with compassion for those who are hurting.

And that's another reason why I'm so happy to be writing this foreword — because that wisdom and compassion come from the heart of my son, Robert A. Schuller, the book's author. Of course, Robert is much, much more than just my son. He is also the pastor of Rancho Capistrano Community Church, a rapidly growing congregation in San Juan Capistrano, California. As chief executive officer of several church-related organizations — a retreat center, a retirement community, a preschool program, and others — he has proven himself to be a more than capable administrator.

But what makes me proudest is that Robert has a heart for people. He wants to see people everywhere living in peace, freedom, and joy — the kind of life that God wants for all of His people. His book is going to help a great many people take some important steps toward finding that type of life.

As a pastor, I see this book as a great source of hope and encouragement for people in need of recovery.

As the father of the author, I see it as a great source of pride!

Robert H. Schuller

1
The Power of Recognising Your Powerlessness

John C. took his first drink in 1942. And he liked it. He liked it very much.

Thus began eight years of dependence on alcohol, eight years of life on the edge of destruction, eight years of hurting himself and those who loved him the most.

You wouldn't know any of that if you met John C. today. He's a successful businessman, an articulate, well-groomed gentleman whose love for life is immediately apparent.

John C. has managed to become all of these things because he hasn't had a drink in more than 40 years. In fact, he can tell you the exact date of his last drink: August 16, 1950. He can also tell you the time: 7 P.M. It was on the day after that John encountered the power of God through a Twelve-Step program, and his life was totally, dramatically, and irrevocably changed.

John can trace his problem with alcohol to an earthquake that devastated Compton, California, back in 1933, when he was eight years old.

"It was a really bad one," he remembers. "And the night of the earthquake we all slept out in front of the house in a tent. We were afraid to go back inside."

The young boy could hear men and women wailing and screaming up and down the street, as the town continued to shake throughout the night and much of the next day.

Before the earthquake John had been secure in a world where all adults, and especially his parents, were in control of things and would make sure that no matter what happened everything would turn out all right. The earthquake changed all that.

"I saw that adults really didn't have control, and it was traumatic."

His feelings of insecurity were compounded by a difficult relationship with his mother, whom he remembers as "a real worrier."

He recalls, "I was really uncomfortable as a teenager, and as soon as I was old enough I enlisted in the navy." That's when he had his first drink, and "it made me feel like a secure little kid again. I loved it."

As the years went by, he continued to love it because it helped him to block out all of the bad things in his life. It also contributed to his doing quite a few bad things, such as stealing and engaging in illicit sexual affairs — but his drinking didn't allow him to spend much time thinking about those things.

For awhile.

After eight years of alcohol abuse, John C. found that drinking didn't seem to help him anymore. It just compounded his worst feelings. He didn't know what to do and contemplated suicide. Meanwhile, he just kept drinking.

And so it was that on a hot August night in 1950, he found himself sitting in a bar in his hometown of Compton, holding a drink in his hand.

"I knew I had to do something .... so I put that drink down when it was still half full, walked out of the bar and went home." He had no idea where he got the resolve to walk out of that bar. The next day he drove to the city of Long Beach to a club where he knew the local chapter of Alcoholics Anonymous met and sat there for the entire day. That night he attended his first meeting of AA and heard, for the first time, about a Twelve-Step program that could set him free.

"I was a mess," he remembers. "I really was."

He didn't like all of the men he met at that meeting, especially one tough, bespectacled old bird named Carl who had a very sharp tongue. Ironically, Carl later became John's sponsor in AA. John did enjoy hearing the spoken testimonies of the men who had found sobriety through AA.

"They looked so happy and were so proud of the fact that they weren't drinking anymore. It really looked good to me."

So he went back to the next meeting. And the next. He began to work the Twelve-Step program in earnest. And he set out on the road that took him from being a no-account drunk who was in trouble with the law, to being a sober, respected, contributing pillar of his community.

As I said, he hasn't had a drink now in more than forty years — and he is quick to give credit, first to God, and then to the Twelve-Step program that AA introduced to him. He says, "I have a great knowledge of the fact that God has taken care of me and will continue to do so."

He also says, "If anyone could go back and see the way I was drinking, and then see how much my life has changed... well, I don't care what his life was like, he'd have to know that it was possible for him to change, too."

The Twelve Steps Are for You

Right now you may be saying to yourself, "Well, that's an inspiring story, and I'm glad John C. was able to put his life back together. But what does that have to do with me?"

Probably quite a bit.

My experience as a counsellor has shown me that most human beings have incorporated dangerous and destructive behaviours into their lifestyles. Some people recognise these dysfunctional behaviours and know they need to change them. Others may be aware that something is out of sync somewhere, but they choose not to think too much about it. Then there are those who absolutely refuse to admit that they have the slightest problem in their lives.

If you've ever attended a meeting of Alcoholics Anonymous, you know that as the recovering alcoholics introduce themselves to each other, they say, "My name is ______, and I'm an alcoholic." They do that for a very good reason: The admission that a problem exists is the very first step toward peace, healing, and freedom.

Ask a practising alcoholic if he thinks he has a drinking problem, and he'll probably say something like, "Of course not. I just have a few drinks now and then." Unfortunately, as long as he has that attitude, he'll never get the help he needs — and he'll go on hurting himself, his family, and everyone else he loves.

Perhaps you are beginning to recognise that you have a problem with alcohol or some other substance or habit. If so, you can be set free, just as John C. was. In this book, I am going to present you with a Twelve-Step plan that can bring you freedom.

May be you're ruining your body with drugs (and I'm referring to everything from hard drugs and cocaine to pot and diet pills and all that's in between). If so, keep reading, because I'm talking to you, too.

Do you want to give up smoking because you know it's killing you, but you just can't seem to do it? Read on — because help is available.

I am also talking to you if you are:

- An overeater, bulimic, and/or anorexic.
- Addicted to illicit sexual behaviour.
- Addicted to gambling.
- Struggling with co-dependency.
- Wrestling with compulsive and harmful behaviour.

This is also addressed to you if you have incorporated behaviours into your lifestyle that cause you to:

- Isolate yourself from others.
- Sabotage relationships you really want to hold on to.

- Alienate people by being too controlling or possessive.
- Spend all of your time trying to please others, with the result that they walk all over you.
- Be afraid to enter into new situations or meet new people.

If you have any of these problems, or any similar problems, this book is for you. It will help you understand *why* you behave the way you do, as well as *what* you can do to eliminate harmful behaviours and attitudes from your life.

If you don't really see any significant problems in your life, I still recommend this Twelve-Step program for maintaining your peace and achieving spiritual growth.

Recently I delivered a series of messages at Rancho Capistrano Community Church in California. It was titled, "Twelve Steps for Spiritual Growth." I talked about the critical importance for us as individuals to acquire wholeness and wellness in our spirits, souls, and in fact our entire beings.

This series of sermons has had a tremendous impact on the congregation. I have seen many people's lives changed dramatically for the better, and other people start out on the path that is going to bring dramatic change to their lives. In the first few months of the series I saw four people face up to their drinking problems and enroll themselves in an alcohol-treatment program. Several stopped smoking. Three others are dealing with the problem of co-dependency. Another is seeking help for an eating disorder. Throughout the entire congregation, there is an attitude of openness, forgiveness, and an air of excitement.

All of us feel the good changes that are taking place — both in our life as a church, and in our lives as individuals.

That comes as no surprise to me because, like John C., I have seen time and again how these steps can bring peace and healing; how they can lift the brokenhearted out of the depths of despair, failure, and depression; and how they can help to put broken lives and broken families back together.

The bottom line is, these Twelve Steps work. But in order for them to bring about necessary changes in your life, you have to do more than just know what they are. You have to put them into practice, and this book is going to help you do just that.

Here are the Twelve Steps for Spiritual Growth:

1. I will admit that I am powerless over my hang-up and that my life is unmanageable.
2. I will acknowledge that God is greater than I and that He can bring restoration to my life.
3. I will turn my life over to God.
4. I will make a searching and fearless moral inventory of myself.
5. I will admit to God, myself, and another human being the exact nature of my wrongs.
6. I will make myself entirely ready to have God remove any defects from my character and bring about the necessary changes in my life.
7. I will humbly ask God to remove my shortcomings.

8. I will make a list of the people I have harmed by my past behaviour and become willing to make amends.
9. Wherever it is possible, I will make direct amends to the people my behaviour has harmed.
10. I will continue to take personal inventory of my life on a regular basis and promptly admit it when I do something wrong or lapse back into old behaviour patterns.
11. I will seek to know more of God.
12. I will seek to carry to others the glorious message of the possibility of a spiritual awakening.

In my role as a counsellor, I find that far too many people in today's world are living what Henry David Thoreau called "lives of quiet desperation."

They are:

- Disconnected from their past.
- Fearful of the present.
- Terrified of the future.

You may very well see yourself in that brief description — or at least the way you feel much of the time. If that's the case, please keep reading because we are going to undertake a journey that will bring you to the place where you are:

- Connected to your past.
- Living contentedly in the present.
- Hopeful about the future.

It may not be such an easy thing to finally be at peace about the things that have happened to you in the past, but with God's help it can be done. It may take some effort to make peace with the present, as well, but you can get to the point where you realise that even the present cannot separate you from God's love. And, when it comes to being hopeful about the future, you will find this much easier to do when you understand for certain that God really does love and care about you and that He wants only the best for you.

The Power of Powerlessness

Now let's take a look at the first of these Twelve Steps.

I will admit that I am powerless over my hang-up and that my life is unmanageable.

What are the implications of admitting that you are powerless over your problem? When I think about someone who admits that he is powerless over addiction and that his life has become unmanageable, I hear in my mind someone whispering a prayer. I hear someone weeping and saying, "Lord, I have failed. My life isn't what it should be. So, God, please take me as I am. Heal me, touch me, make me whole."

The person who comes to that recognition and who prays that prayer has taken the first major step toward living the justified life. And that can also be considered the "just-as-if-I'd" life, as in, "just as if I'd never sinned," "just as if I'd never been violated," or "just as if I'd never become tangled up in this lifestyle."

Prayer takes many forms. Sometimes it's nothing more than an inner recognition of need — of powerlessness and reliance on God's power in any given situation. Other times prayer takes the form of heart-to-heart communication with the Creator — speaking to Him in your thoughts. And then of course, there is audible spoken, prayer.

It's this last variety of prayer that, a few years ago, got me through a difficult time with my daughter Christina, who was not yet two years old. She had been playing on the swing in the backyard when she fell and hit her head — hard. She cried a bit, but with the resilience of most children her age, quickly forgot about her "boo-boo" and wanted to get back to play.

Later that day, my wife Donna and I discovered a bubble about the size of a walnut on the side of her head. Naturally, we were frightened. We took her to the doctor, where X-rays revealed that she had a skull fracture. The bubble was caused by spinal fluid seeping from the fracture. The doctors told us that Christina needed to have a CAT scan so that they would have a better idea of the extent of the damage and what needed to be done to repair it. Because Donna was pregnant and couldn't expose our unborn baby to the radiation involved in the procedure, I was elected to help our little girl get through this procedure.

Now, if you've ever been through a CAT scan, you know that you have to be as still as you can be sometimes for a rather long time. In Christina's case, they told us she'd have to be perfectly still for at least four minutes — and that's pretty close to an eternity to an active toddler.

You probably know that a CAT scanner looks something like a giant donut. There's a hole in the middle, and whatever needs to be scanned is placed in this hole. As I watched, my little daughter's head was slid into the hole. From the top of the donut hung a roll of tape that was supposed to attract her attention and keep her quiet during the procedure.

Christina was perfectly still as she lay there, looking for all the world like a little angel, clutching her blanket and her bottle. But I knew very well she wasn't going to stay that way for four minutes, and if anyone thought that roll of tape was going to hold her attention... Well, all I can say is that they didn't know little girls very well. Or at least not mine.

But I had an idea. "Christina," I said, "let's pray." We had just taught her to pray, and every time she did she closed her eyes and remained perfectly still. Obediently, she folded her hands over her chest and closed her eyes. As she did so, she bit down hard on her bottle — she wasn't going to take the chance of losing that precious possession.

I prayed, "Dear God, thank you for Mommy and Daddy and Angie and Bobby and Christina." We went through all the family members and then I said, "Amen."

That was the wrong thing to do, because as soon as she heard that word "amen," she knew the prayer was over, and that meant it was time to get up and play. Thinking fast, I said, "Oh, and dear God, thank you for Christina's blanket, and her bottle, and..." As soon as she heard the words, "dear God," she got back in her "prayerful posture" with her little hands folded, her eyes closed and her body perfectly still. And all the while, the CAT-scanner was whirring away, giving the doctors an up-close look at my little girl's injury.

Well, in four minutes' time, I think I prayed for every bit of Christina's anatomy, starting at her feet and working my way up to the top of her head, especially praying for the "bump" on her head and asking God to make it better. I started my prayerful journey with "thank you for Christina's toenails" and ended with "thank you for Christina's hair." And you know what? It worked. In more ways than one.

Not only did Christina lie perfectly still and allow the CAT scanner to do what it needed to do, but it also happened that God answered my prayers regarding her skull fracture. She didn't require surgery, the fluid dissipated, and today she is perfectly happy and healthy.

I was facing two situations in which I felt completely powerless. First, I was powerless in the face of my daughter's injury to her head. Second, I was powerless in the matter of getting her to stay still for four minutes so the scan could be done properly. The power of prayer came through in both of those difficult situations.

God Will be Powerful for You

It is really only when we face up to our own powerlessness that we allow God to be powerful for us. And it is only when God is powerful for us that we can gain the victory we so desperately need. The Bible tells us that the strength of God is made perfect by our weakness. In other words, as long as we're going through life thinking that we're self-sufficient, that we're capable of doing everything on our own, our best attempts are quite likely to fall short. But when we learn to acknowledge our own powerlessness in certain situations and rely on the power of God, that's when great things are going to happen.

I've known many people who have gone through life thinking that everything was on their shoulders. Whatever was going to happen, they had to make it happen. Their own success, or failure, depended entirely on their own actions. What a terrible way to live!

The reality is that one of the most liberating moments in your life may be when you realise that you truly are powerless. That frees you from the burden of having to do everything "your way." It allows you to let go of your burdens and let God carry them for awhile. It lets you off the hook and makes it possible for you to be gentle with yourself. You've seen the bumper sticker that says, "Let go and let God," and I think that's a very good idea.

Here's another way of looking at your life:

No God = No Peace
Know God = Know Peace

This is important enough that I can't overemphasise it. Facing up to your own powerlessness does not mean giving up in your struggle to overcome. It merely means giving up trying to do it on your own and being willing to let God help you.

One of the best ways I know of to learn to rely on the power of God is to spend time meditating on some of the promises that are contained in his Word. You may have seen those little "pocket promises" booklets. They are a great source of encouragement. Desk calendars with a scripture for every day of the year are also helpful in reminding us not to rely on our own power but on the power of God.

How can you *not* be encouraged when you read verses like Isaiah 41:10: "Do not fear, for I am with you; do not be dismayed, for I am your God. I will strengthen you and help you; I will uphold you with my righteous right hand."

Jesus himself says, "In this world you will have trouble. But take heart! I have overcome the world."

Think about this. Would you be interested in going to God while you are confident in your own power? Absolutely not. Only when you come to the end of your self, when you have discovered your own powerlessness, will you be willing to come to God for rest. Only then will you find the peace that comes from resting in His power.

He Came to the End of His Rope and Found Himself

I opened this book with the story of my good friend John C. He is one of the most "alive" people I have ever met. He is enthusiastic, he is contented with his life, he is wealthy — and as far as the world is concerned, he is an extremely powerful man.

If you knew John C. today, you'd never think, even for a moment, that he is someone who tried many times to overcome the power the bottle held over his life but just couldn't do it. That's exactly the way it was until he realised that he was powerless in the face of his addiction and quit trying to do everything on his own.

John C.'s life took a dramatic 180-degree turn, and the same thing can happen to you. He found power in powerlessness and you can too.

Is there a difficulty standing in front of you, defying you to deal with it? Are you thinking: "I can't possibly handle this"? Well, you're right. In your own strength, you can't. But with God's help, you can overcome! So get ready, because a change is going to come! A wonderful change!

During the next few days, spend some time meditating on some of God's promises that are found in the Bible. And remember, though you may be powerless to overcome your problem, "With God all things are possible!"

2

God Will Restore You

Every Sunday morning I stand before several hundred people at the Rancho Capistrano Community Church and preach a sermon. It's something that comes fairly easily to me, and I enjoy giving my people something to take away with them, something that will help them as they deal with the daily pressures and stresses of life in this world.

You might think that it's always been easy for me to get up in front of a group and speak. After all, I grew up watching my own father speak before hundreds, thousands, and, via television, millions of people every week. You might think that watching him in action would have made me comfortable with the idea of public speaking.

If you had that impression from watching me speak to my congregation or on television or by considering my background, you would be way off the mark. When I felt that God was calling me into the ministry, I was terrified at the thought of speaking in public. The very idea made my hair stand on end and gave me goose bumps, and yet the call was so strong and so unmistakable, there was no way I could resist it. I knew there was only one way that I could ever hope to follow the call and overcome my fear, and that was with God's help.

My fear of speaking in public was always so bad that when I was a boy in school I used to sit in the very back corners of the classroom, because then there was less chance that the teacher would call on me, and so I felt safe. Sometimes, when she asked a question, the other kids would raise their hands as high as they could, straining and stretching in an effort to get the teacher to call on them so they could show off what they knew. Not me! I was more apt to pretend to drop my pencil on the floor and bend over to pick it up — just to make sure she wouldn't call on me. On the rare occasions when my name was called, my voice would crack, my knees would shake, and I'd feel perfectly ridiculous.

This fear of speaking in public even followed me into college. I started college with a major in vocal performance, but I was too terrified to perform. That's one of the main reasons for changing my major during my junior year to ancient civilizations, a division of the classics. As one of my electives I took speech — not because I wanted to but because I knew that, sooner or later, if I were going into the ministry, I was going to have or get over my fear of speaking in public. My teacher was generous enough to give me a C, but the truth was that I couldn't bear to speak in front of the group. It didn't matter how much time I spent researching my topic and preparing myself. I fell apart when time came to translate all of my preparation into an actual speech.

One time, when I visited some relatives in Missouri, I was asked to deliver the message at their small church. I remembered my father telling me about his first preaching experience. He had prepared a twenty-point message because he had to speak for twenty minutes, but when his twenty minutes in the pulpit were up, he had only addressed his first four points. He had said to me, "Robert, don't make the same mistake I made. It takes more than a minute to cover a point."

And so, for my message at this small Missouri church, I prepared a five-point message. But my message didn't last twenty minutes as I had planned. I had completed the entire sermon in just five minutes — and had nothing more to say.

It certainly didn't seem that I had been called to be a preacher, and yet God wouldn't let go of me. He wasn't loud or demanding about it, but it seemed that He kept whispering in my ear, telling me that He wanted me to preach. This was the biggest problem in my life, and I was absolutely hopeless in the face of it. Did I pray for God to help me overcome my fear? You bet I did. But whatever progress I made was painfully slow. I was definitely not a chip off the old block! To be completely honest about it, I was afraid of failing God, and I felt that it was entirely up to me to overcome my fear. I wanted so hard to change but just couldn't seem to do it.

And then one day something amazing happened.

My father and I were supposed to speak before a women's group that was meeting in the Crystal

Cathedral. Prior to the service, he sat down with me and we went over the outline we had prepared. As we did, I felt the same old anxiety, the sense of dread and fear. But what happened was that as I opened my mouth to speak, the peace of God seemed to descend upon me. It happened in an instant — one of the greatest feelings I've ever experienced. Not only was I not afraid, but I was actually enjoying myself. I knew that God had restored me, and that He was supplying me with His own power.

From that moment on, it's been rare when I've been afraid to speak before a group. If I am in a class and I have a question, I raise my hand and ask it. If I am in a group discussion and believe that I have a comment or an insight that will help the other members of the group, I give it freely. I know without question that on that particular day in the Crystal Cathedral I received a gift from God that enabled me to overcome the greatest obstacle in my life. There is no other way to account for what happened and for the change it brought to me.

It could be that you're saying, "Okay, Robert, that's fantastic for you. But you don't understand. The problems I've got are so much deeper, so much worse than that." In some ways, that may be. But let me assure you that there was an incredible agony in realising that God had called me to preach and knowing that speaking in public was very nearly the last thing in the world I wanted to do. God helped me to overcome my fear. He gave me restoration. He can and He will do the same thing for you.

Acknowledging that fact is the important second step in becoming the person you want to be.

I will acknowledge that God is greater than I and that He can bring restoration to my life.

Needed: An Understanding of God's Love & Care

In the last chapter we talked about the importance of recognising the fact that you are powerless before God. Sometimes that's bit easier than moving on to the second step and acknowledging that God is willing to bring about restoration.

Oh, we know that He is capable of bringing about restoration, but we just doubt that it's something He wants to do. We tend to shrug our shoulders and say, "Why would God want to do something like that for me? He has better things to do with His time and energy, doesn't He?"

That sort of attitude betrays a lack of understanding of god's nature. The Bible tells us over and over again that God is loving and kind. And His love is not just extended to the human race as a whole. He loves you and me as individuals and is willing to demonstrate that love, if we will only let Him.

Far too many well-meaning parents have done a good job of "putting the fear of God" into their children, but they haven't helped their children learn about His love. I have counselled many people who grew up with the notion that God is some kind of cosmic drill sergeant who goes around with a notepad, giving demerits any time anyone does anything wrong. You might say He is a lot like Santa

Claus — "making a list and checking it twice; gonna find out who's naughty and nice" — only He isn't as much fun as Santa, and He seems to take delight in recording our failures rather than our successes.

What a perverted picture of the Creator of the universe! No wonder so many people have the idea that God isn't interested in helping them out of their present difficulty. They think that He stands scowling and shaking His finger at them because they got into that difficulty in the first place!

But it just isn't so!

It is true that God has given us His laws in His Book, but He didn't give them to us because He's a spoil sport who wants to keep us from having fun. Just the opposite is true. He gave us His laws because He is the one who created us. He knows what's best for us. He wants us to have happy, productive, contented lives and He knows what that takes.

For example, one of God's laws concerns sexual love. God created sex, and it's good. It's good because it is a means by which one man and one woman are able to give themselves completely to each other, thereby "becoming one flesh." It is the deepest union two human beings can experience. It is also good because it is the means through which children are born and the human race is perpetuated. And it's good because it is a pleasurable experience.

God could have made sex something that was difficult, or boring, or just totally unpleasant, but instead, he made it something wonderful. He also made it very clear that this was an experience that was to be shared by a man and a woman who had committed their lives to each other. Sex is something sacred and He expects us to treat it that way. Why? Because He knew what would happen to us if we began thinking of sex in a cavalier manner. He knew there would be damage, both psychological and physical.

If you don't think that sexual promiscuity brings psychological problems, you should spend a few weeks in my office, listening to some of the people I counsel and hearing firsthand what happens to people who think they are "liberated" sexually.

The potential physical damage is obvious — there's syphilis, and gonorrhea, and herpes, and AIDS. In 1991, AIDS became the number one killer of those between the ages of twenty-four and forty-four in Orange County, California.

I've heard some people say that AIDS is a plague from the hand of God and that He sent it to punish us for our sexual misconduct. AIDS is *not* a punishment from God, but God knows the course of nature. He put it in motion and sustains its movement. Because He knows what will hurt us, He told us what to do and what not to do. In His wisdom, He knows that treating sex in any way other than that for which it was intended will be harmful. He has warned us that bad things will happen if we don't listen to him, but many people react in total disobedience — like children who think they know more than their parents and wind up in deep trouble.

So don't think for a moment that God's laws are meant to punish you or keep you from having fun. Rather, they are to protect you and give you a fulfilled life. If you break them, however, you are bound to be hurt. That's the way nature works. Even though God is forgiving, nature is unforgiving. If you jump off a twenty-story building to commit suicide and decide on your way down that you're sorry for what you've done, God will forgive you, but nature will not.

That's the law of gravity. Why did God build it into His universe? Because it keeps all the planets in a fixed position, rotating around the sun. Without gravity, the earth would go spinning into space, and we'd all freeze to death in a very short amount of time. Well actually, we really wouldn't have to worry about that, because without gravity, we'd all go floating off on our own, bouncing around through space like so many helium-filled balloons. So gravity is good, and yet that same gravity is going to hurt anyone who takes a flying leap off the Empire State Building! So you see how another one of God's laws is going to help you if you live in obedience to it but hurt you severely if you try to defy it.

As I mentioned earlier, some people grew up in homes where God was depicted in a very negative light, where fire and brimstone were the order of the day. No wonder, then, we have so many people who have rebelled against God completely, and no wonder there are organisations such as Fundamentalists anonymous, which are designed to help people overcome the psychological damage that such an upbringing may have inflicted.

If that's the way it was with you, then you definitely need to spend some one-on-one time with God, praying and meditating. I also recommend a delightful little book by J.B. Phillips, *Your God Is Too Small*.[1] In order to overcome the problems that are keeping you in bondage, you have to understand that

God is powerful and that He loves you and is anxious and willing to use His power to help you be an overcomer.

Take the First Step

It is important to know, too, that the way God usually works is that He waits for us to take a step in the proper direction and then supplies us with the power we need to finish the journey. Understand, though, that the motive is extremely important. It's not a matter of taking the step and thinking, "I'm going to do this by myself," but a matter of stepping out in faith and trusting God to make up what we lack in ourselves.

One of the greatest people I have ever had the privilege of knowing was Corrie ten Boom. You may have read her life story, *The Hiding Place,*[2] or seen the motion picture that was based on her book. If you are not familiar with Corrie, let me just tell you that when she was a young woman in the Netherlands, her homeland was occupied by the Nazis. When it became clear that Hitler was trying to exterminate the Jews, her devoutly Christian family took it upon themselves to hide from the Nazi authorities as many Jews as they could. Thus, they converted one of the rooms of their house into a "hiding place."

Unfortunately, the secret was eventually discovered, and all of the members of Corrie's family were sent to concentration camps. By the time the war ended, Corrie was the only one still alive. Far from being angry or bitter toward God, Corrie came out of the Nazi hell determined to spend the rest of her life spreading the message of his eternal love — and that's exactly what she did until her death a few years ago.

One of the stories I heard "Aunt" Corrie tell many times was of how her father always gave her the money she needed when she had to take a train trip somewhere. "But, he would never give me the money for the train until I was ready to go," she said. "In fact he would always wait until just a few moments before I left, and then he would give me the amount I needed to get on the train and get to where I was going."

That's the way God is with us. We have a will, we have a desire, we know where we are heading, but we say, "I don't have the talent to do this or the ability to do that." Suddenly, though, when the time comes and when we're in the proper position, able and ready to receive, God infuses us with His power and enables us to get the job done.

The Truth Will Set You Free

I'm constantly amazed by people who won't put their trust in God but will put it in other things. Here in California, for instance, I'm always reading about some celebrity who is changing the spelling of his or her name or making some life-changing decision, based on advice from an astrologer or "personal psychic." That's really sad because it is turning away from, rather than toward, God. God alone holds the keys to the future, for all of us!

Why do we turn away from God? Some of us have felt that we've been let down. We've tried things and we've failed. We've seen loved ones die — parents, brothers, sisters, spouses. Some of us had big expectations for our lives when we were younger, but now that we're getting older we see that things are not turning out the way we hoped they would, and that leaves us disappointed and bitter.

When things go wrong, it helps to have someone to blame. When no one else is handy, it's convenient and easy to point the finger at God. But He's not the one who is responsible for any of those things. He desires only the best for you. Tragedy may come into your life because that's just a part of living on planet Earth, but if you will turn your sorrows over to him and trust him, God will make something beautiful even out of those tragedies and failures.

When you acknowledge his power and his intention to help you, you can even begin to look at occurrences that are less than pleasant in a new light. For example, I heard about a farmer in Washington who was especially proud of the apples he produced every year, and with good reason. His farm was at a high elevation, and the cold winds that came through there made his apples especially crisp and flavourful. Every year, after he harvested his crop, he would polish those apples until they virtually shone. Then he would put them into beautiful packages to show them off. These weren't your ordinary run-of-the-mill apples but the kind that made beautiful gifts to send loved ones for Thanks giving and Christmas. As word of his marvellous apples spread, it got to the point where he was inundated with orders even before he had harvested the fruit.

One year, just before harvest time, a severe hailstorm pummelled his property. When it was all over, there wasn't single apple without blemishes on its skin. There was nothing wrong with the apples. They just didn't look as pretty as they usually did, and the farmer was afraid that the people who had ordered them might be disappointed and ask for their money back.

Then he had an idea. He took all of the apples with the little blemishes on the outside and wrapped every one of them the same way he did every year. He put them in the same kind of packages. Then he added a note. It read: "Notice these high-quality apples. This year represents the finest crop. You can see the blemishes caused by the hailstorm, which created the extreme cold giving the ultimate flavour and ultimate crispness to these apples."

Well, not a single order was returned. In fact, just the opposite happened. The following year when his orders started coming in he had many requests from people who wanted to make sure they got the apples with the blemishes this year, too!

My point is that when you are living daily with an understanding of God's love, care, and guidance, you begin to realise that all things do work together for your good — that even the "blemishes" serve to make you a better, stronger, more capable person.

And so it is true: When you know the truth of God's concern for you, you definitely will be set free. There's not a single doubt about it.

It's Never Too Late

It doesn't matter how many years you've been struggling to break free from whatever it is that holds you bound. It could be that you've had a secret problem in your life for twenty years, thirty years, even longer. The length of time you've struggled doesn't diminish God's power or take away from the fact that He loves you and wants to see you set free.

It doesn't matter how many times you've tried and failed or what others have said to you or about you. God knows you better than anyone else. He knows you even better than you know yourself, and He says that you can succeed — and with His power, you can.

I recently came across a list of people who were dismissed as failures at some point in their lives. That list encouraged me, and I'm sure it will do the same for you. These were people who refused to give up but kept on moving in the direction of the goals they had established for themselves, and by the grace of God they eventually reached them:

- Winston Churchill was considered "washed up" after committing what everyone agreed was a tactical mistake during World War I.
- Lucille Ball was told early in her career that she had absolutely no ability as an actress and that she should forget about show business, go home, and find a nice man to marry.
- Zane Grey was told by a publisher, "You can't write; you'll never be able to write," and to please quit wasting the publisher's time with his "rubbish."
- Beethoven had such difficulty learning to play the piano that his music teacher gave up on him.
- Thomas Edison was considered a dunce by his elementary school classmates and the grades he received supported their evaluation.
- Louis Pasteur received a failing grade in chemistry class.
- Abraham Lincoln failed at almost everything he tried — business, politics, and law — before he was elected president in 1860.

This list could go on for several pages with names of great, successful people — but people who, for at least part of their lives, were not considered great or successful by anyone's measure.

Whatever your life has been so far doesn't have to say anything about what it will be in the future. Past failures don't mean there won't be future successes. You may be in bondage today, but that does not mean you won't be free tomorrow.

How to Obtain Faith

Taking this second of the Twelve Steps is really nothing more than a conscious decision — a decision to acknowledge the power and grace of God. Sometimes it's not so easy to get to the place where you can make that decision. How can you grow in faith? How can you begin to believe that God is there for you and that He is willing to help you?

Here are five things you can do:

1. Ask Him to give you this sort of faith.
2. Spend time in prayer every day.
3. Meditate on the Scriptures.
4. Take the time to "stop and smell the roses."
5. Spend time with others who have faith.

First of all, there is nothing wrong with asking God to give you faith.

In the ninth chapter of Mark, there is the story of a man who came to Jesus, seeking healing for his son. When the Lord challenged the man to have more faith, he replied, "I do believe; help me overcome my unbelief!" Far from rebuking him, Christ responded by healing his son. He will respond positively when you sincerely ask for a stronger faith.

The second thing you can do is to spend time in prayer. As you talk to God about the things that are going on in your life, you will get to know Him better, and the better you know Him the more you will understand His power and His love. Further more, as you take your requests to Him, you will begin to see how He is working things out in many of those areas, and your faith will be strengthened. In other words, as you become more and more able to trust Him with the smaller details of your life, you will also become more and more able to trust Him with the bigger matters.

Meditating on Scripture is the third thing you can do to build your faith. It was discussed in some detail in the first chapter, so I won't spend much time on it now, except to say that there is a difference between reading a scripture and meditating on it.

You can sit down and read a chapter or two in five minutes without really giving much thought to what you're reading. But when you meditate on it, you let it soak in to the point where it becomes real to you, and you can feel the truth of it.

For example, consider the Twenty-third Psalm. It's one of the first Psalms children learn. It's fairly easy to memorize, and it's beautifully written. But there's much more to it than just beautiful words.

> The Lord is my shepherd, I shall not want.
>   He makes me lie down in green pastures,
> He leads me beside quiet waters,
>   He restores my soul.

Your faith can't help but be built up when you meditate on these beautiful words. The Psalm tells you right off that the Lord is your shepherd. What does that mean to you? It means that He will gently and lovingly lead and care for you. The shepherd doesn't drive his sheep along with a whip. Instead, he walks in front of them, showing the way, and because they know him, the sheep follow along behind.

And then the Psalm tells you that the Lord, your shepherd, will give you what you need so you "shall not want." He will give you "green pastures" in which to lie down.

You are not getting the full impact of the promises of the Bible if you merely read them. Instead, you need to spend some time "bathing" in them. When you do, they will infuse you with faith.

The fourth item on my list of things you can do to increase your faith is to "stop and smell the roses." What do I mean by this? Simply that it is a good idea, every now and then, to call a time out from the hectic pace of life, slow down, and take a look around you.

These are hectic, harried, hassled times. Modern technology was supposed to make our lives easier, but in many ways it has added to the frenetic pace of our lives and has been the source of stress piled on stress. Too many of us are living life at an unhealthy pace — with computers, faxes, microwaves, and the like enabling us to rush through days, weeks, months, and years. And when you are moving through life at ninety miles per hour or faster, it is difficult to see God's hand at work.

So, stop! Look at the beauty that God has put into his creation. Consider the delicate structure of a rose. Take a walk, just at the end of the day, and let yourself be swept away by the beauty of a sunset. Better yet, take a day or two away from your daily grind and go to the beach, the mountains, the desert, or the forest — anywhere you can get in touch with nature and with the God who created it all.

Not too long ago, there was a movie called *Grand Canyon*. At the end of the film, several people who live in the middle of Los Angeles make a pilgrimage to the Grand Canyon. The closing scene is of all these people standing and looking out over the vastness of the canyon, drinking in its majesty and beauty, and letting it restore their souls. Now the movie didn't say anything about God. It didn't even hint at the fact that the beauty we see around us comes from the hand of our Creator. The message it presented is still a good one; namely, that our troubles can seem insignificant when we put them alongside the glory of the world that surrounds us.

I would take things a step further than the film did, though, and say that our troubles can seem insignificant when we compare them with the majesty of a God who cared enough to build spectacular things into our planet — things like canyons, mountains, beaches, deserts, and flowers — and who gave us gifts like sunsets and full moons and the scent of honeysuckle floating on a summer breeze.

God's loving care is all around us, but in order to see it, we have to look. And for many of us, in order to look, we have to slow down. So if you want to increase your faith in the ability of God to help you overcome the problems you are facing, open your eyes wide and look at the evidences of His power and His love that are all around you.

The fifth thing you can do to increase your faith in God's power to help you overcome is to spend time with others who have faith. It's good to share with those who are moving along with you on the journey toward wholeness and with those who are a bit farther along the road who can say, "Yes, God can do it for you, and I'm proof of that!"

In the Genesis account of the creation of man, after God Created Adam, he said, "It is not good for man to be alone." It wasn't good then, and it's not good now. God doesn't intend for us to try to make it through life without support from other human beings. The old song says that "People who need people are the luckiest people in the world." Truly, though, there are no people who don't need people. God expects us to lean on one another, encourage one another, and "carry each other's burdens". This is true in the world at large. And it's especially true of people who are striving to live lives of faith.

You need to have a friend you can talk to, and better yet, several friends. These friends can be people from your church, your social club, your neighbourhood. It really doesn't matter, but they need to be people with whom you can share your victories, your failures, and your fears; people who will encourage you and do their best to understand what you are going through; people who will give to you and allow you to give to them.

One of the many reasons why Alcoholics Anonymous is so successful is that it utilises the support of the group. It's not easy for someone who is craving a drink to stay away from alcohol, but it's made easier if that person knows he's not alone. Have you ever tried to lose weight? It's much easier if you have a partner who is trying to lose weight right along with you. And then, when you're tempted to fall back on your unhealthy eating habits, you think, "No, I'd better not do that." Part of it is that you don't want to let your partner down. Part of it is that you don't want to be embarrassed in front to her. The third thing that enters into the equation is that there is strength in numbers.

Another way of fellowshipping with others is reading the autobiographies of people who have been where you are right now — or some place very similar — and who have, with God's help, emerged victoriously. Reading inspiring books and magazine articles can be extremely helpful.

In the days just ahead, work on building up your faith. Work on getting to the point where you can say with deep conviction, "God is greater than I and He can bring restoration to my life."

When you've done that, you're ready to move on to the third step on the road to a renewed life.

3

Turn Your Life Over to God

During the winter of 1991, a man by the name of Saddam Hussein led his country into a tragedy of horrendous proportions. Hussein was foolish enough to believe that tiny, ill-prepared Iraq — its already inadequate resources depleted after a decade of war with neighbouring Iran — could take on the military might of the United States and her allies. He will, thus, go down as one of the greatest fools of the twentieth century.

Even as allied planes continued to pour devastation on Iraq, Hussein refused to surrender. The result was that his nation was almost totally destroyed and thousands upon thousands of Iraqi soldiers, perhaps more than 100,000, died. By the time the war finally ended, some members of the allied forces were openly expressing their sympathy for the Iraqi soldiers, who were totally hopeless in the face of allied might. They were dying by the thousands, they had no hope at all of winning the war, and many of them were without food, shoes, and even the ammunition necessary to make a small show of resistance. Even so, Saddam Hussein refused to surrender, forcing them to keep fighting, and the slaughter continued.

Some of those Iraqi soldiers had a better idea. They laid down their weapons and walked into the open with their hands held high, surrendering to the allies who were advancing toward their positions. The strangest thing about the way they surrendered was that they didn't act as if something terrible were happening to them. Instead, they embraced their captors. They seemed almost happy that they were getting the opportunity to surrender. And, surely, in many instances they were happy.

They were happy because they knew that, for them, the fighting was over and their lives would be spared. They were hungry, injured, and poorly clothed, and so they were happy because they knew that their captors would feed them, provide medical care and see to it that they were properly clothed. In short, they thought that their "enemies" would take better care of them than their own country had. They weren't walking into hell. They were walking out of it.

It would have been totally absurd for them to keep on fighting. Fighting for what? For nothing more than the continuation of a repressive regime that kept its grip on power only through the constant threat of torture and terror.

Are You Still Fighting?

In a spiritual sense, there are millions of people in our world today who are in the position of those

Iraqi soldiers before they surrendered. They're getting pounded on all sides. They're bruised and bleeding. Still, they refuse to lay down their weapons and surrender. May be you're one of these people. If so, you need to take a moment and ask yourself a very important question: "What am I fighting for?" Another question to consider is: "Whom am I fighting against?"

You probably don't even realise it, but chances are very good that you are fighting against God Himself. Just as the Iraqi soldiers had no way to win the war against the United States and her allies, there is no way you can win if you are fighting against God! The ironic thing about it is that God doesn't want to fight at all. He's on your side. He wants to help you, but He can't do it until you put your weapon down and say, "I surrender." That brings us to the third of the Twelve Steps on the journey toward wholeness.

I will turn my life over to God.

To turn your life over to God implies a surrender, a decision to quit trying to get by on your own power and to let God lead and empower you. This step is the turning point — the corner-stone on which all else rests. If you do not make the decision that you will "let go and let God," then you might as well resign yourself to a life of struggle and disappointment and forget about the other eleven steps.

The first two steps did not demand that you make a decision. The first one merely required you to face up to the fact that you are powerless against your problem. The second step involved giving intellectual assent to the idea that God is able to bring restoration to your life. Now, you have to take things a gigantic step further and make a conscious decision to give up control of your own life and let God take over.

This is not an easy thing to do. The natural tendency of all human beings is self-centeredness and self-will. It's hard to give someone else, even God, control of your life, but it can be done. When you do it, the door is opened for you to receive tremendous benefits.

Always Remember: Father Knows Best

One thing we always need to keep in mind is that God is smarter than we are. We know what we want, but He knows what we need. In many ways, we can be like undisciplined children, running after things we shouldn't chase and reaching for things that will hurt us if we actually manage to get our hands on them.

My daughter Christina is a bright, intelligent, energetic little first grader. She has always been inquisitive and self-sufficient. I cannot remember at time when she didn't want to "do it myself." In many ways that's a fine quality, but for a child her age, parental guidance is usually necessary to keep her out of trouble. Even when she thinks she can handle something herself, she may be wrong.

I remember one such occasion. She was two years old. She had a sore throat. Instead of telling Mommy or Daddy, she decided to take care of it herself. She climbed up to the medicine chest, took out the children's Tylenol, and started helping herself to the candy-flavoured drug. When her mother discovered what she was doing, she had already taken several tablets. Following our pediatrician's advice, Donna gave Christina ipecac syrup to make her vomit. Within minutes she regurgitated everything in her stomach and continued to have dry heaves for the next hour — the cure was definitely worse than the sore throat, and she hasn't attempted to take any medicine on her own since. It was because Christina thought she knew best that she got herself into trouble.

My point is that earthly parents usually know what is best for their children, and our heavenly Father always knows what is best for us. He knows that giving in to our childish demands is not what we need. When a parent does what is best for a child, that child may sometimes think that mom or dad is being mean or unreasonable. When God does what is best for us, we may sometimes feel the same way. But if we are patient and have confidence that what He is doing is entirely for our benefit, we can also know that sooner or later we will see the reason He acted with us as He did.

Not long ago my son Anthony, who was three at the time, was invited to a birthday party at a Chuck E. Cheese's restaurant. If you've been there, you know what a crowded, noisy, frenetic place it can be. Anthony, feeling like a big boy, was insistent that we not walk him into the restaurant and help him find his friend's party. He wanted to do it by himself.

It took about twenty minutes for us to drive from our home to the restaurant, and all the way there he kept saying, "Don't come in with me. Okay, Dad? Just drop me off at the front door. Okay, Mom? Let me go in by myself."

As you might expect, Donna and I were not at all happy about that idea. In fact, our first inclination was to say absolutely not, but it was so important to him that we finally gave in. We decided that we'd let him go in by himself, give him a couple of minutes, and then follow him, just to make sure he had found the right party.

The parking lot was busy, so, although it wasn't easy, we talked him into allowing us to walk him at least across the parking lot and to the front door of the restaurant. When we got to the front door, he put his hands up in a "halt" stance and announced, "Okay, now you stay here. I'll go in by myself!"

Donna and I looked at each other, and then she said, "Okay, Anthony. Have a good time."

Carrying his beautifully wrapped present and grasping a string that was attached to a blue helium-filled balloon, which floated over his head, he marched into Chuck E. Cheese's. We watched him disappear into the restaurant, and although I can't speak for Donna, I know I felt as though I were watching my little boy march off to join the Marines!

The next two minutes passed very, very slowly, but finally we figured that enough time had gone by that it wouldn't embarrass him too much if we went in to check on him. We would just find the party, say hello to the birthday child, and find out what time we needed to be back to pick up our son.

When we walked into the restaurant, I couldn't believe how crowded it was. I had seen it full of people before, but never like this. It was packed! I knew right away that there was no way short of a miracle that Anthony could have found his way to his friend's party. In fact, my first panicked thought was, "How in the world are we going to find him in this crowd?"

Then Donna saw something: that little blue balloon, floating above the crowd. There, beneath it, was our little boy, whose eyes were now about the size of Frisbees. He hadn't known what he was getting himself into, and even though the little guy would never admit it to us, he was frightened. When he saw us, those big, round eyes lit up, and a huge smile spread across his face. "Mommy, Daddy, I can't find the party! I can't find the party!"

"That's okay, Anthony. We're here. We'll help you find it."

Finally, we found the right group of children, said hello to the birthday girl and her parents, and made our exit. By the time we left, Anthony was playing so happily with his friends that he didn't even notice we were leaving. The importance of walking into the party by himself had long since been forgotten. Our presence hadn't really embarrassed him at all.

As Donna and I drove home, I thought about how often we all act the way Anthony did when it comes to God's help in our lives. We don't want His help. We want to do it all by ourselves. When it comes to God, we don't mind His being with us when we're sitting in a pew in church, but we don't want anything more than that.

"Okay, God, I'm cool. I can handle this by myself. You just stay in church where you belong. Well, may be you can walk me to the front door, but that's all."

I don't mean this to sound judgmental. I assure you, I have played these games with God myself. I have tried to shut him out of my life in certain situations and circumstances, and I've acted as though I really didn't need him. But you know what? I always found out later that I was wrong. God's power isn't confined to the walls of the church. He's the power behind everything we see. He's the one who created the entire universe, even those billions and billions of planets and stars that Carl Sagan is always talking about. As powerful as He is He cares about you as an individual, and He wants to infuse your life with His power. As far as I can see, it makes no sense at all not to allow Him to do that.

You've Got to Push the Button

Several years ago, I had the opportunity to travel to Egypt and take a cruise down the Nile River. The cruise came to an end when we came near the area of the great Aswan High Dam. I do not use the word *great* lightly. This is a huge dam — one of the largest ever constructed. It took eleven years to build and holds back 200 billion cubic yards of water. There are twelve turbines spinning, and they produce 12 billion kilowatts of power annually. That's a tremendous amount of power.

When construction of the dam was completed in 1972, Egyptian President Gamal Abdel Nasser was on hand for the dedication. He had the privilege of pushing a button that started those huge turbines spinning. As they began to turn, electricity was generated and began flowing through the power lines. It went out from the dam and fed the cities of Egypt, Sudan, and surrounding territories.

The power was available because there was water to force these turbines to turn. It wasn't until the button was pushed, however, that the turbines began to spin and the power began to flow.

Our lives are very much like that. We have the ability to "push the button" and allow the power of God to flow into our lives. God is there. He's all-powerful. He's willing and anxious to use His power for our benefit, but He can't do a thing for us until we push that button. How do we do that? By surrendering our lives to Him, by a conscious act of the will that says, "God, you're in charge here now. I've acknowledged that you have the power to restore me. Now I'm turning myself over to you and asking you to do what you need to do to bring about that restoration."

I've had people tell me they were afraid to turn their lives over to God. Either they were involved in something that they didn't want to give up and were afraid God would make them give it up, or they were afraid God would make them do something that was totally disagreeable to them. This isn't the way God operates. "For I know the plans I have for you,' declares the Lord, 'plans to prosper you and not to harm you, plans to give you hope and a future".

God doesn't get upset or angry when we ask Him to come into our lives and take charge. The reverse is true, in fact. In the third chapter of the last book in the Bible — the Revelation of John — Jesus is described as standing at the door and knocking, waiting for us to open up and let Him in. That's a picture of an active, aggressive God who wants to help us overcome, not a God who *might* be grudgingly willing to help us.

God wants you to surrender your life to Him because He wants you to live in joy and be fulfilled. Without His presence in your life, that's just not going to happen. God wants every bit of your life.

Hold no problem back,
    Nothing large, nothing small.
When God says, "surrender,"
    He wants it all!

Some people think that God is only interested in "spiritual matters," and that these spiritual matters don't have any relationship to day-to-day life in the physical world. Wrong! God is interested in everything we are and do.

Surrendering to God involves giving Him not only your problems and worries but also your ambitions, abilities, talents — every aspect of your life. In return, you will get a chance to start over in life, with all the stains and rips from unpleasant experiences repaired! This is what it means to be born again: to be washed and cleansed from sin and made as pure as a baby. There's no other way that can happen — no other way to start over — except by the grace of God.

Surrender Is a Constant Process

A word of caution is in order, though. I do not believe that surrendering to God is a once-in-a-lifetime process. It's something we need to do again and again on a daily basis. As various situations arise, as we encounter temptations to fall back into old patterns and lifestyles, we need to decide again and again to give the matter over to God and respond in the way He directs us to respond.

Some people teach that when you surrender your life to God, He immediately changes your personality and your character so that you are no longer interested in those "worldly" things that caused you so much pain in the past. That's not the way it usually happens. Instead, you will need to surrender your will to his again and again, and as you do, He will give you the grace and power to get through the moment. Surrender is a constant process.

In the first chapter, I told you the story of my good friend John C., a man who was addicted to alcohol for eight years but hasn't had a drink since 1950. It may surprise you to hear this, but he still attends meetings of AA on a regular basis — twice a week. Why? Because he wants to make sure that he keeps up his resolve. Some things have to be done again and again and again, and resisting temptation is one of those things. So is surrendering to God.

What if you fall short of what you know God wants for you and of what you want for yourself? Don't be too hard on yourself. Failures and relapses are common. No human being has ever been perfect (with one exception). When slipups come, you can rest in the knowledge that these, too, are covered by the grace of God. As soon as you turn over even your failures to Him, you will grow in His grace and power. Then, those failures and relapses will come less and less frequently, and your life will be more and more what you want it to be.

Please remember that you can't play games with God. He knows what's going on; you can't keep anything from Him. He knows you better than you know yourself. In fact, if you are really serious about turning your life over to Him, He may reveal some things to you that you'd rather not see, or that you wish you didn't have to confront. As I've said before, it's only when you face up to the truth about your life — the total truth — that you can be set free from the things that bind you.

When I think about being set free through knowing the truth, I think of my own wonderful wife, Donna. It has been only over the last few years that she has been able to face up to certain truths about her life. Donna would be the first to tell you that many of the things that happened to her when she was a girl have profoundly affected her life as an adult. As long as she was unaware of the significance of childhood events, or as long as she did her best to keep them buried, she could not come to grips with or modify the adult behaviours that so troubled her.

Donna remembers, for instance, that her mother and father fought regularly. Dinnertime, especially, was an unhappy occasion, and it was rare that the family got through a single meal together without some kind of explosion. She remembers wondering if all parents fought the way hers did.

Looking back, she says, "I never realised how deeply I was affected until I had a real problem handling dinnertime with my own children. It seemed to me that they were always acting up at dinner and I was always tense and nervous."

Sometimes she'd get into an angry, defensive mood when she was cooking dinner. "The kids weren't really acting bad," she remembers. "They were just being kids, but I couldn't handle it."

By the time Donna was a teenager, she realised her family was more chaotic than some of her friends' families, but she didn't feel that she could talk to anyone about what went on behind the closed doors of her house.

When she was twelve, her mother and father separated, and although she and her younger brother stayed with their mother, they often visited their airline-pilot father on weekends — at least, when he was in town. Before long, however, because she was at the age where she was interested in going to dances on weekends and doing things with her friends, her weekend visits to her father became fewer and farther between.

One Friday night, when she was thirteen, two of her friends spent the night, and she remembers having a great time laughing and carrying on until well past midnight. Even so, the next morning, her mother woke her up much earlier than usual. Right away, Donna knew that there was something hanging in the air. She had a sense that something was wrong.

Two people sat on stools in the kitchen, talking quietly to each other. Donna wondered why people had come to visit so early in the morning and also why they were talking in such quiet, subdued tones.

Donna's mother led her into her brother's bedroom, sat the two of them down on the side of his bed and said, "I have something to tell you that's going to hurt you for a long time. Your dad was killed in a car accident last night."

While Donna and her brother sat there numbed by the news, she went on to explain that he had been on his way to the airport when a car ran a red light and broadsided him, killing him instantly. This was a version of the story created to "protect" the children. The truth was that Donna's father had been drinking and that his drinking had contributed to the accident.

The loss of her father only added to Donna's inability to cope with life. She began to drink heavily herself. Two and a half weeks after her father's death, Donna's mother remarried. During the wedding, Donna and a friend spent the day sneaking the champagne that was left in glasses after the traditional toast to the bride and groom. It was enough to get them drunk.

When she was still in junior high school, she and her friends would fill baggies with booze from her mom's liquor cabinet. Then they would stash them in bushes, where they would be available for the Friday-night dances. She remembers poking around in the bushes, trying desperately to recall where some of those baggies were hidden.

Eventually, she even married a man with a past remarkably like her own, a man who liked to drink as much as she did. The marriage lasted only three years, and Donna says it is fortunate for both of them that they didn't drink themselves to death. "We almost destroyed each other," is the way she puts it.

Drinking was only one of the problems that Donna was dealing with, and it would be years before she began to be set free. Freedom came through two means. First, she faced up to the reality of the past and understood how the things that had happened when she was a girl had affected her. The most important lesson that she learned is stated by John Bradshaw in his book *Homecoming*[1]. "That which is not worked out will be acted out." In other words, you must face up to the reality of the past — instead of remaining "disconnected" from it — and come to grips with how the things that happened in the past have affected you. If you don't, those past events are going to manifest themselves in ways that won't be good for you or for other people in your life.

For example, by her own admission, Donna was irritable and a nervous wreck every night at dinner. Only when she understood the source of that behaviour, was she able to begin to effectively deal with it.

I want to talk more about this in just a moment. But first, here's the second means by which Donna obtained her freedom. She gained a better understanding of the power of God to set the captive free. As a girl and a young woman Donna believed in God. She knew He was out there — somewhere — but she really didn't understand that He cared for her personally or that He was interested in helping her overcome the fears and problems that kept her bound.

In Donna's case, the primary problems within her family were made worse by alcohol abuse, and so some of the problem areas she has had to work on in her own life have had to do with the dynamics surrounding alcoholism. Although alcoholism is more immediately obvious than some other dysfunctions, it is only one of many addictions that is used to cover up pain and divert feelings and that can tear a family apart and damage a child for life.

I've already mentioned a couple of problems that Donna had to overcome, but there were others. Some of these you many recognise from your own life.

Guilt

Donna felt guilty most of the time. If there was something wrong, Donna had a hard time believing it wasn't her fault. She was usually ready to take the blame. The two words she said most often were, "I'm sorry." She felt responsible for the fact that her parents fought most of the time and ended up living separate lives. She felt that if she had been staying with her father on the weekend he died, he would have been at home instead of out on the highway. In other words, in some ways she felt responsible for his death. She had to come to realisation that she wasn't really to blame for many of the things she felt guilty of, and she had to realise that forgiveness and absolution were available for the things she was guilty of.

Afraid to Trust Feelings

Donna was afraid to trust her feelings. This is another thing you learn when you grow up in a home that is affected by alcoholism or some other addictive disease. Why? Because you look at what is going on in your family and you think, "something is wrong here," but Mom and Dad make believe that everything is really fine and expect you to do the same thing. The unspoken message is, "Oh, don't worry about this. This is normal and happens in all families." The child in the dysfunctional family doesn't see this type of thing happening in other families, however. That gives him two choices: He can either trust his feelings and decide that Mom and Dad aren't exactly telling him the truth. Or, he can decide that the problem lies with the way he sees things, because he surely must be mixed up. Most children tend to think that the problem lies with them, rather than with their parents. Then as adults they don't trust their own perceptions and are afraid to let others know what they're thinking. They usually won't give an opinion on an issue until they find out what everybody else thinks about it.

Trying to Learn the Rules

Donna couldn't figure out the rules. Life is very unpredictable for the child who has an alcoholic parent (or a parent who is impaired by some other addiction or difficulty). The dysfunctional family is never at peace because what is perfectly acceptable behaviour one day may be the cause of "all hell breaking loose" the next. As a result, the child grows into an adult who has great difficulty setting reasonable limits for his own behaviour — commonly referred to as boundaries. He has a hard time saying no, for instance, because he's never been quite sure when he needs to say no. He has a hard time deciding what he should and shouldn't do, and he always has the sinking feeling in the pit of his stomach that whatever he's doing, it's wrong.

Not Trusting Others

As an adult, Donna found that the lack of trust she had felt toward her parents as a child was projected onto other people. She had a hard time believing people, especially people who cared about her and tried to express the way they felt. Because of the way things had always been in her family, she couldn't fully commit herself to people. She was sure they were going to let her down. She needed constant reassurances, but sometimes all of the affirmation in the world wasn't enough for her to let her guard down.

Rigidity

Donna was rigid in her perceptions of her own role in life. Now this may seem like a contradiction, especially since we've already mentioned that the child from a dysfunctional family has a hard time figuring out what the rules are. Even though that's true, the child also has a very narrow view of how he relates to others — of his role in their lives. In other words, he holds tightly to his perception of his own place and his own life, and he's afraid to expand that view. Frequently, these children grow into adults who want control over people and situations, as was the case with Donna.

In her family, Donna saw herself as the peacemaker and at other times as the invisible child. Wherever there was smoke, she would rush to the scene and do her best to put out the fire. Because she wanted so much for things to be smooth and peaceful, she ran away from a confrontation, even when a confrontation was what was needed. She was like the character Charlie Brown, in the "Peanuts" comic strip, who believes that no problem is so big or so great that it can't be run away from.

Donna carried into adulthood the misconception that as long as there was peace, everything was fine. Unfortunately, the world doesn't work that way, and the person who believes in "peace at all costs," usually finds himself bulldozed by someone who's a bit more forceful.

He lacks respect for himself, and therefore others don't respect him either. My point is that the adult child of an alcoholic has a hard time being everything God intends him to be, simply because he sees himself in such narrow terms.

Donna says that her relationship with God has helped her immensely in recognising the existence of these problems, being willing to discuss them openly, and battling to overcome them.

She acknowledges that it wasn't easy, at first, to begin opening up and telling people about her past. For one thing, Donna is a pastor's wife, and I'll be the first to admit that's one of the toughest jobs around. In far too many churches, pastors' wives are expected to be impossible combinations of Joan of Arc and the Virgin Mary. Because of that, Donna was afraid that if she told people the truth about her past, they would think she wasn't worthy of her position.

Instead, Donna says she has found that people in general seem to respect her more for opening up and talking about her past. They don't see her as some "perfect" creation of God but as a real person to whom they can more easily relate.

She has admitted to me that when we were first married she was afraid she couldn't measure up, that she couldn't be the pastor's wife that people would expect her to be, so she tried to keep her mouth shut and just "go with the flow."

Now, she looks for ways to help other pastors' wives deal with the problem areas of their lives. "Too many of them have a lot of things they're trying to bury way down deep, and it's made them miserable," she says. "They're afraid of being honest with themselves and facing up to the truth. The very thing they're afraid of would give them the freedom they need so desperately."

Donna reminds me that people who are ashamed of themselves have a difficult time believing that God loves them. Because that's true, it's imperative to deal with the shame of the past and move on into a future full of God's love and power.

It's ironic, perhaps, but the only way to gain freedom is to dig all those old, unpleasant things up, see them for what they are and then turn them all over to God. Learn to live in the present and have hope for the future. Only when you have turned your whole life over to Him — including all of those things that you find shameful or hurtful — can He make something beautiful out of it.

I want to close this chapter with a prayer. I hope that when you read these words, you will do so with feeling, meaning what you say.

Please, pray with me.

Heavenly Father, thank you for your love, for your grace, and your power in my life. I give myself to you completely, realising that it is only through your power that I can be complete. Cleanse me, Lord. Keep me from things that are harmful to me and harmful to those I love. Guide me in the days and weeks ahead. Strengthen me so that I can do what is right. I welcome your power into my life.

Amen.

4

Through the Magnifying Glass

Are you familiar with the story of Peter Pan? I remember as a little boy, being thrilled when Peter Pan overcame Captain Hook and his renegade crew of Pirates. My own children have been captivated by that story just as I was all those years ago. (Well, not that many years ago!)

But here's something you may not remember. What was it that first brought Peter Pan into Wendy's bedroom? Was he:

a. a homeless child looking for a warm place to spend the night?
b. a burglar looking to steal something of value he could pawn?
c. looking for his shadow?

If you picked c, you are right. What happened is that Peter Pan's shadow had run away from him and he was trying to track it down. It wasn't easy because the elusive thing was flying all over the place in an effort to stay free, but Peter finally caught it, and when he did, Wendy sewed it on for him. Peter

Pan knew he wasn't a whole person unless he had his shadow with him.

You and I are just like Peter Pan in that we, too, need our shadows, or at least we need to understand them. Remember that the shadows of your life are not your enemies. They are part of you. They are things that happened to you early in life, and the behaviours and attitudes that you built into your life in response to these things were for protection, probably when you were a child. Back then, these behaviours enabled you to survive and cope with the situations you encountered. Now that you are an adult, they are no longer helpful, and they may, in fact, be harmful to you if you don't deal with them. You may pretend they're not there, but they are, and they may be the root of all sorts of dysfunctional behaviour. Only when you realise that you have these shadows can you learn to deal with them. Meanwhile, you can do your best to ignore them, but that won't-make them go away. Even though you may forget about these shadows, you catch a fleeting glimpse of some of them from time to time. They flutter around like ghosts in the subconscious.

Each one of us has his own secret little treasure box and inside are all those shadows: the things that happened to us when we were children; the way we were brought up; the problems, frustrations, and troubling thoughts we have to deal with on a regular basis; the inadequacies we feel as individuals; the problems we face with a dysfunctional life. The list could go on and on. There comes a point when we have to come face-to-face with these shadowy things. They may be frightening, but if you can learn to look at them as teachers, you can learn all about yourself, and they will thus benefit you rather than harm you.

It's been nearly forty-five years since my friend John C. has had a drink. Surely, after all that time, he can no longer be considered an alcoholic. Surely it would be all right for him to lift a glass of champagne in a toast at a wedding or have a glass or two of wine with dinner. But John won't do either one of those things. Why not? Because he understands himself. He knows his own weaknesses — the shadows of his life — and he is determined not to give in to them.

As he says, "You can't begin to think that you can take another drink successfully. If you get to that point, that's when you can get yourself right back into trouble."

You see, John C. knows two things very well. He knows the power of God, and he knows the weakness of his own nature.

We've been talking quite a bit about the power of God. Now it's time to change our focus and think about step four.

I will make a searching and fearless moral inventory of myself.

One of the challenging things that we have to do if we want to grow spiritually is chase down our shadows. We have to find those parts of our selves that we've allowed to run away, that we've buried, that we don't want anybody else to know about. What we want to do is find out what's right — what's wrong — with the things we do and what's behind the way we relate to life. Then, having a better understanding of why we do what we do, we can ask God to help us deal with the things that hold us back, eventually removing destructive behaviours from our lives.

Most of us may be able to make a "searching moral inventory," but it's probably not going to be done "fearlessly," since the majority of us have at least a few skeletons hidden away in the various closets of our lives. What I mean here by "fearless" is a self inspection that will leave nothing hidden and that will have the aim of getting at the truth, the whole truth, and nothing but the truth, whatever that truth may be.

I'm not going to tell you to find reasons to blame other people for the ways you feel and behave; nor am I going to tell you to accept the blame for everything yourself and let everyone else go free. The goal is to discover the truth, no matter how much that truth may hurt — or how much it may please us.

Many people know the Robert Burns poem, "To a Louse," which was allegedly written after he saw one of the insects crawling across the back of an elegantly dressed and very snobbish woman.

> Oh wad some power the giftie gie us
> To see oursels as others see us!

I feel certain that Burns was correct in his assumption that most of us would modify our behaviour if we could see ourselves the way others do (i.e., as we really are). That's because some of us see ourselves as better than we are, and others of us as worse than we are. Step four is designed to help us see ourselves as we really are, so we can then begin to work on changing those things about us that need to be changed.

Have you ever realised, after an evening of being with friends, that you had something stuck between your teeth the entire evening? Perhaps it was a tiny little bit of green spinach — a tiny little bit that seemed about a mile wide when you finally saw it in the mirror. That sort of thing has happened to just about all of us at one time or another. So, what happened when you first saw that speck of spinach? I'll tell you. Your mind flashed back to what you were doing all evening. There you were, talking and laughing with your friends, and all the while they were thinking, "Boy, he sure looks dumb with that thing stuck between his teeth." (At least, now that you've looked in the mirror and have seen it for yourself, you're pretty sure that's what they were thinking.) You wish somebody had been kind enough to tell you about it but no one did; so there you were, Mr. Green Teeth. There's nothing you can do now but smile and forget about it, but how you wish you had looked in a mirror earlier in the evening! If you had, then you would have seen the spinach yourself, removed it, and spared yourself a great deal of embarrassment.

What we're doing in this fourth step is holding up that big, full-length mirror to ourselves and examining our reflected image in minute detail — with a magnifying glass, even. It is not easy to do that, but it is always very much worth the effort. There will probably never be anything more difficult for you to deal with honestly than these shadows of your life. If there is not total honesty, however, there can be no clarity of mind, and if there is no clarity of mind, there can be no restoration.

For example, remember how my wife, Donna, always saw herself as the peacemaker. In her childhood this was a behaviour she adopted in order to cope in a family that was often torn by the angry strife between her mother and father. As an adult, however, there were many times when she needed to stand up for herself — when a confrontation would have been very much in order — but instead, she gave in to what someone else wanted. So great was her desire to be the peacemaker that she was more than ready to submit her own feelings and needs so she could be the doormat for whoever wanted to walk on her! Only when she confronted that old peacemaker shadow from her childhood was she able to work on modifying her behaviour in a way that was better for her, as well as for other people — such as her children, who sometimes needed her to be "tough."

It was another shadow that caused her to have such a hard time dealing with dinnertime. Realising why she felt and acted the way she did enabled her to overcome the inappropriate feelings and reactions.

Three of the Most Dangerous Shadows

There are many different types of shadows and many responses to them, but some responses to experiences in our lives are particularly dangerous and must be dealt with before we can deal with any others.

Three dangerous responses are:

➢ Unawareness (sometimes referred to as denial)
➢ Resentment
➢ Fear

In just a moment, we're going to get down to the basics of preparing your personal inventory, but before you look at all the other areas of your life, you must examine yourself for this terrible triumvirate.

Unawareness

Unawareness is something you may have developed as a child to protect yourself by helping you believe that things were better than they really were. In Donna's case, being unaware let her think that all parents fought the way hers did, that her dad didn't really have a drinking problem, and that it was okay if he only drank beer.

Unawareness can become a serious problem for an adult who uses it to cover his failures, as in: "Oh, I only have a drink or two to unwind at the end of a hard day." "Addicted? Nonsense. I can quit anytime I want to." "Oh, come on! Everybody I know does this sort of thing."

Being unaware can take several forms:

Pretending. A person may pretend something didn't happen when he may or may not be aware that it did. This person is like the child who has fallen and hurt himself but he laughs and says, "It doesn't hurt at all," because he's afraid of going to the doctor.

Blaming others. The person who blames others doesn't deny that he has done (or is doing) something wrong, but he says it's all somebody else's fault and refuses to take responsibility for his own actions.

Making excuses. There is a great deal of difference between an excuse and a reason. A reason is the truth, whereas an excuse is a lie — a false front behind which to hide the truth.

Beating around the bush. The person who is adept at staying unaware always wants to talk about things later but never manages to get around to it.

Going on the offensive. Have you ever had someone turn the tables on you by getting angry before you had a chance to be angry yourself, or before you had a chance to question him about something? That's what I mean by "going on the offensive," and it's an excellent diversionary tactic if you want to stay away from admitting your problems.

Do you recognise any of these traits from your own life? Be as honest as you can, and remember that this is all part of taking a fearless moral inventory of yourself. A person who lives his life unaware of his shortcomings is a person who refuses to grow.

Resentment

Resentment is the second of the three most dangerous shadows, and it's a problem because it can keep a person chained to the past so that he cannot move into the future. Resentment says: "I can't help the way I am, and it's all my mother's fault." "If only my father had treated me better, I wouldn't have all of these problems today." "My life has been nothing but one bad break after another, so I just refuse to try anymore."

Any or all of the above statements may be true, but even so, holding onto anger and resentment hurts you and nobody else. There is a saying that "living well is the best revenge." While I don't particularly like the idea of revenge, I do like the living well part. In other words, the best thing to do is to say, "Sure, life has been unfair sometimes. Some people I trusted have let me down. I've been hurt and bruised in the past, but that has no bearing on my life today or tomorrow. I'm going to live life to the fullest anyway. I'm not going to let yesterday's hurt control my life forever."

If you hang on to your resentments you are consigning yourself to a lonely, bitter life and running the risk of developing serious emotional problems.

When I think about resentment, the old joke comes to mind about the man who was bitten by a rabid dog. As the doctor came into the emergency room to treat him, the man was writing furiously in a notebook. Reassuringly, the doctor put his hand on the fellow's shoulder. "You don't have to write out your will," he said. "You're not going to die."

"This isn't my will," the man replied. "I'm just making a list of all the people *I'm* going to bite when *I* have rabies!"

You may know some people like that, who are full of resentment toward others. You may even see your own attitude in that story.

Fear

Fear is the third shadow that needs to be dealt with right away. Fear keeps a person from taking an honest look at himself. It keeps him from responding appropriately to situations that might be perceived as threatening. It keeps him from honestly telling others how he thinks and feels.

It's not easy to admit that you're afraid. It's an admission of weakness, and that's something our society frowns on. It's when you're weak, though, that God's strength can really come into your life.

Resentment and fear can combine to keep a person paralysed. Resentment keeps him chained to the past, and fear keeps him from moving into the future. If you want to know what part fear and resentment are playing in you life, just ask yourself some questions about specific people. Is there someone you resent? A parent? Your boss? An older brother or sister? A spouse or ex-spouse? Similarly, is there someone or something you fear?

Then, after you've identified sources of resentment and/or fear in your life, ask yourself how such feelings have affected you. Have they lowered your self-esteem, caused you difficulty in establishing relationships, caused you to feel constant anger? Only when you've identified these shadows and the feelings they cause, can you deal with the feelings. If you realise you have resentment against people, it's time to move from that to forgiveness. If you have identified fears in your life, it's time to face them with the courage God gives. Being freed from resentment and fear is like coming out of prison!

The Apostle Who Saw Himself

If I asked you to name the chief of the Lord's apostles, whom would you pick? I know whom I'd choose, and I feel confident that you'd pick him, too.

My choice would be Peter. Of course, I realise that all of the apostles were equal in the eyes of the Lord. Christ himself stressed that on many occasions. He reminded the Twelve that the one who wanted to be the leader of all must be the servant of all. There was no room for lording it over others or for worrying about who was number one. Still, Peter's credentials for being considered the chief apostle are very impressive.

Peter was the decisive one, always quick with an answer, always ready to act first and think about it later. On the Day of Pentecost, he boldly preached the first-ever Christian sermon, and he continued preaching boldly until, as church history tells us, he was martyred by being crucified upside down (after having asked his captors not to crucify him in the usual way, since he did not consider himself to be worthy of dying in the same manner as his Lord).

There is no doubt that Peter was a mighty man and that the Christian church owes him a great deal. I believe that Peter never would have been able to do the things he did without two spectacular failures that prompted him to see himself clearly and thereby come to understand that he wasn't nearly the supersoldier for God that he had thought he was.

In the first incident, the apostles were out on the lake in a boat, when Jesus came to them, walking on the water. Naturally, they were terrified when they first saw a ghostly figure moving toward them on top of the waves, but when they realised it was Jesus their terror turned to awe. Then Peter, true to form, told Jesus that he wanted to get out of the boat and walk on the water, too.

Jesus answered simply, "Come."

At first, Peter was doing all right. Even though there was nothing but water beneath him, every time he put his foot down it felt as solid as a rock. Then he began to be distracted by the wind and the waves and to think about how ridiculous it was trying to walk on water. The next thing you know, he was sinking.

Of course, Peter was rescued, but I have a feeling that he said very little the rest of the night. For one thing, he had to be embarrassed by what had happened to him. For another, I'm sure he was thinking about the lack of faith he had displayed, reminding himself of all the spectacular things he had seen the Lord do and making up his mind that would be the last time he was ever going to doubt like that. But it wasn't.

The next time it happened was at Jesus' trial. Peter was at least brave enough to be waiting outside in the courtyard while the trial was in progress but certainly not brave enough to try to go inside and testify on behalf of his teacher. In fact, he wasn't even brave enough to let anyone else know why he was there, or that he even knew Jesus at all. On three occasions, people recognised him as being one of Jesus' disciples, but when they asked him about it, he denied it. He denied it with such vehemence, in fact, that he punctuated his words with swearing and cursing.

Immediately after the third time that he denied he knew Christ, Peter was jarred to the terrible reality of what he had done by the bombastic sound of a rooster crowing. When Peter heard that rooster crow, he remembered the words of Jesus: "I tell you the truth, this very night, before the rooster crows, you will disown me three times".

Then he went out and wept bitterly. Yes, Peter was crying because he realised that he had let the Lord down, and Jesus knew in advance that that was exactly what he was going to do. He was also crying because he had seen himself so clearly. He knew, at that instant, how weak he could be and how far he had to go to be the sort of man he wanted to be.

That was undoubtedly the low point of Peter's life, at least as far as his self-image was concerned. But it was also the turning point. That bit of introspective weeping, coupled with that sinking experience out on the Sea of Galilee, helped Peter sort things out. It was at this point in his life that he successfully resolved to strengthen what needed to be strengthened and to weed out what needed to be removed.

It was painful for Peter to see himself as he really was — very painful — but only after that happened was Peter able to become the force who helped to build the early church and who boldly preached the good news of Christ's resurrection, in spite of tremendous opposition and persecution. Only then was he able to fulfil the words of Christ: "I have prayed for you, Simon, that your faith may not fail. And when you have turned back, strengthen your brothers".

Your Personal Inventory

It's true that you can't get to where you want to be unless you know where you are right now. And you can't know where you are right now without taking "a fearless moral inventory."

Have you ever wondered how a boat, far out on the ocean, can find its way back to the safety of the harbour? After all, out there on the water there are no discernible landmarks, no mileage markers or highway signs to look for. So how does the captain know how to head straight for home? He is aided by an ingenious device called a loran. The way it works is that there are two radio waves that cross at a certain point, and the loran gives the exact location of the boat with reference to those radio waves. Once the captain knows where he is, it's a simple matter of getting out his navigational charts and setting his course for home.

You may feel like a boat on the water right now, adrift and not at all certain of the direction of the harbour. The first thing you need to do is find out where you are. One of the tools that will aid you in this discovery is a personal inventory of your life.

In order to prepare this inventory, you need to find a time and place where you can be alone with your thoughts. My suggestion is that you take at least an hour a day for as long as it takes and write down all of your personality characteristics that you can think of. Don't think you can complete a "searching" inventory in twenty or thirty minutes, or even in a couple of hours. Take the time you need to do this right and you will achieve maximum benefit from the process. There are weekend retreats that help people work on step four. If you are able to go away by yourself for a couple of days, so much the better. If you have some favourite "thinking" place, somewhere you go to get away from it all, that would be ideal.

It is also a good idea to pray about it, asking God to reveal things to you that might otherwise stay hidden. Ask him to help you be completely honest with yourself and to give you clarity of mind so you can think things through.

There are certain behaviours that are extremely common in adults whose childhoods were spent in dysfunctional families. As you examine your own life, you may want to look especially for the following.

A tendency to isolate yourself. The extreme case is agoraphobia, fear of public places, when a person may be afraid to even leave his house. I remember a woman named Susan who was terribly afflicted by this disorder. Susan was from a very well-to-do family and seemed to be a capable and talented person. She was married to a man who was successful and respected in the community; they had a good marriage and everything seemed to be going her way.

But then, in 1971, an earthquake measuring 6.4 on the Richter scale hit her home town of Simi Valley, California. That quake threw Susan into her downward spiral.

She remembers, "Every time I would leave the house I would start having anxiety attacks. My heart would start pounding, I'd break out in a cold sweat, and I had to get out of wherever I was." The first time she had one of her panic attacks, it was because she felt trapped in an elevator. The second time she heard some rolling thunder, which sounded ominously like the noise an earthquake makes. Then the attacks started coming without cause or warning.

Finally, she was completely housebound and held captive by fear.

Looking back on it now, she realises that her fears were compounded by the fact that when she was a child, her mother was drinking.

How did Susan overcome her fear? She says the first step was beginning to watch *The Hour of Power* on television. Through that program she received faith and hope and realised that she could succeed in life. She joined a support group, got professional therapy, and slowly but surely began facing the real world again. If you knew Susan today, you would never guess that she was once a literal prisoner of her own fears. This is an extreme example of someone who tried to isolate herself, but her story is not all that uncommon.

How about you? Do you tend to withdraw from others? Are you afraid of venturing out of your comfortable surroundings into the threatening world of interpersonal relationships? If this is your tendency, follow these steps:

1. Look for specific examples where you have isolated yourself. Perhaps a group of friends invited you to accompany them to a movie, and even though you really wanted to go, you were afraid to, so you said no and spent the evening at home by yourself.
2. Once you've seen a tendency to isolate yourself from others, it's time to look for the underlying causes. Write down some of the reasons why you think you behave that way. Seeing those underlying causes written

down in black and white should make it somewhat easier to modify your behaviour. In other words, you'll realise that the sky isn't really going to fall if you accept that invitation next time.

3. Jot down some ways you could modify your behaviour in the future. It could be as simple as deciding that you will not look for a reason to say no the next time someone invites you to go somewhere, or it could be as proactive as inviting some people into your home for a social time.

A tendency to repress anger. Have you ever heard anyone described as a "walking time bomb"? That's the person who goes through life repressing anger. He may deny his anger and act as if everything rolls off his shoulders like water off the back of a duck. But the reality is that the anger is building and building and building to the point where it is either going to be released in one violent explosion or it's going to result in physical damage such as an ulcer, high blood pressure, or deep depression.

Anger is like water building up behind the wall of a dam. In any dam, the floodgates have to be opened occasionally to release excess water. If they are never opened, the water will build up to the point where the dam can no longer hold it back, and the dam will break. In the same way, it is best to give honest and clear expression to your feelings when something happens that makes you angry. Open up those floodgates and let the excess out. Otherwise, it will build up to the point where the dam can no longer hold it back.

A friend of mine, James, had a real problem with anger. He carried resentments toward a father who not only was an alcoholic but had abused James when he was a child and had abandoned the family when his son was no more than seven or eight years old.

James had never been able to find a way to deal with his anger, and the result was that it often erupted in violence and abuse of others. He would even beat his wife from time to time and on one occasion broke her arm.

As time went by and he failed to deal with the issues, he began to deteriorate, not only emotionally, but physically as well. He began smoking more and more, and by the time he was thirty-four years old he was suffering from lung cancer. A year after his first lung surgery, with his anger continuing, his cancer spread to his brain. He finally died at the age of thirty-eight.

If you see that you have a tendency to repress anger, follow the same steps as for isolation.

1. Look for specific ways in which you have recently demonstrated a tendency to repress anger.
2. Try to figure out the underlying causes for your behaviour (such as being afraid to express your true feelings when your were a child).
3. Write down some ways you could have handled the situation better and some things you will do differently in the future.

The tendency to be a caretaker or rescuer. This is especially common in someone who had an alcoholic parent. As a child, this person felt as if he had to take care of that parent. In effect, their roles were reversed, with the child behaving more like the parent, and vice versa.

As an adult, he tends to believe wholeheartedly that he is supposed to be his "brother's keeper," and even though that's not a bad sentiment, he carries it to extremes. This is one of the reasons so many children of alcoholics grow up to marry alcoholics. They are perpetuating their caretaking behaviour.

Incidentally, caretakers often wind up in professions where they can exhibit their caretaking tendencies, for example, as doctors and ministers. You are likely to find caretakers in the church, where they volunteer for every committee in sight because they want so much to help people. The problem is that the caretaker will overdo it if other people are willing to let him. Another problem for the caretaker is that his tendency to always do for and think of others may be the way he avoids looking at his own life.

Examine yourself to see if you have this tendency in your life. If so, how has it been demonstrated in your behaviour? How can you modify that behaviour in the future? No one expects you to completely change your lifestyle overnight. Some of these behaviour patterns are so deeply ingrained that you may have to battle them for quite a while, but admitting that they exist is the first step.

A tendency to hide your feelings. There are two basic reasons why the person who grew up in a less-than-ideal family may have trouble expressing his feelings. The first is that he was afraid of his feelings when he was a child because his feelings told him that things were wrong — not the way they ought to be — and he didn't want to accept that. The second reason is that most likely he was not allowed to express his feelings when he was a child. If he ever told the truth as to how he felt about things, he was told to shut up or was spanked or slapped across the face. So he learned at a very early age to keep feelings to himself. The person who hides his feelings may be smiling on the outside while on the inside he is full of resentment, stress, and anger. As a result, he will have very few honest, deep friendships.

A tendency to need approval from others. The person who never received approval and affirmation from his or her parents is going to seek it from others. This is dangerous territory. There's nothing wrong with wanting to please people or with wanting to have their approval, but there's a great deal wrong with letting the opinions of others determine how you feel about yourself.

This person may find himself running ragged trying to do things for everyone else, simply because he wants them to like him, with the result that a great many people take advantage of him. He or she may become promiscuous — even addicted to sex — in an attempt to gain approval through physical intimacy. In most cases, this happens to those who are trying to gain the approval from others that they were never able to get from their parents. All they find, however, is that others are more than willing to use them, and so the cycle is perpetuated.

A tendency to control. Because the child in a dysfunctional family has little or no control over his environment, he may grow into an adult who tries to control everything, including the behaviour of other people. He can be rigid, unyielding, manipulative, and unwilling to give up what he perceives as his position of authority.

Very often what happens in the life of this person is that he exercises tight control over the "smaller" things because he knows he has no control of the "bigger" things of life. For example, when my wife, Donna, was a little girl, she had no control at all over her parents' relationship, but she could control the way things were in her own room, and so that's what she did. She kept her room extremely neat, never a speck of dust or an out-of-place piece of clothing anywhere.

Donna carried this need to control into adulthood and into our marriage. There was a time when she couldn't stand to have a dirty cup or dish in the sink for more than five minutes. Almost as soon as you had used it, she washed it. In fact, I remember more than one occasion when I was making a sandwich and put my knife down for a moment. When I went to pick it up again, it was gone. She had already grabbed it and washed it — before I was even through using it! She just could not stand any disorder in the world she controlled. The children couldn't leave their toys out. She vacuumed the carpet twice a day. Her life certainly wasn't easy.

I am thankful that Donna was able to work on and conquer her tendency to control, but she understands and feels deeply for those who are still caught up in this behaviour. What this person needs more than anything else is an understanding that it's God who is in control. Once he really understands that, he can relax and let God run the universe.

A tendency to distrust authority. The fear or distrust that developed in this person as a child toward his parents is projected onto others, with the result that he may always feel antagonistic toward bosses, teachers, and other authority figures. He may always think that those in authority are picking on him, putting him down, or that they simply "have it in" for him for some reason. Obviously, a person who can't accept authority will have a hard time functioning in society.

A tendency to have low self-esteem. The person who could never measure up to his parents' expectations is probably going to go through life feeling "inadequate," and "bad." He's afraid to set goals for his life "because nothing ever works out anyway," he thinks he's always responsible when something goes wrong and never responsible when something goes right, and if he should achieve success, he's quite sure it won't last very long. He is very good at magnifying his faults and dwelling on his failures. What he doesn't realise is that we all have faults, and that failure comes to everyone who ever tries anything.

The best cure for low self-esteem is to understand the love of God. He created you in His image. He loves you enough to listen when you pray. He considers you to be somebody important. If He feels that way about you, then you should certainly feel that way about yourself.

This is the last of the self-destructive behaviours I'll discuss here, but as you undertake your "fearless personal inventory" perhaps you will see other areas that need special attention. If any of these tendencies sound like you, investigate further. Look for specific ways that this tendency is exhibited in your life and try to determine what may have caused it. Review incidents and think about how you could have acted differently. You may need help in dealing with a negative behaviour that you identify. Seminars offered by churches or schools can serve this purpose, or you may decide that you need the more intense help available through a counsellor or psychotherapist. Let me urge you again to be as thorough and as honest as you can possibly be.

John Calvin, one of the great theologians of the sixteenth century, said, "In order to come to know God you must come to know thyself and in order to come to know thyself you have to come to know God."

Those words remind me that people come to church searching for the reality and the presence of God, when, at the same time they need to look at themselves and at the shadows of their lives. Only when you fully see yourself can you also see the true reality of God. Knowing God is knowing that He is a God who loves, a God who cares, a God who wants to see you whole and real and complete. That process begins by being totally honest with yourself about yourself.

Finally, before we move on to step five, I want to share these words from the apostle Paul, as recorded in the third chapter of the Book of Colossians, verses 5-10.

> Put to death, therefore, whatever belongs to your earthly nature: sexual immorality, impurity, lust, evil desires and greed, which is idolatry. Because of these, the wrath of God is coming. You used to walk in these ways, in the life you once lived. But now you must rid yourselves of all such things as these: anger, range, malice, slander, and filthy language from your lips. Do not lie to each other, since you have taken off your old self with its practices and have put on the new self, which is being renewed in knowledge in the image of its Creator.

5
The Importance of Confession

The ability to feel guilty can be a good thing — if it doesn't get out of hand. Guilt can serve as a self-imposed guidance system to keep us from doing what we know we shouldn't do.

Imagine what society would be like if there were no such thing as guilt: people doing whatever they wanted, whenever they wanted to do it, without giving a single thought to how their actions would affect others.

It doesn't take too much imagination to picture how difficult it would be to live in a society like that. Guilt is *not always* a good thing, however. It can be very destructive — a load that is impossible to carry, a burden that can cause men and women to stagger far off the path they ought to follow.

The Bible speaks of "godly sorrow," which leads to repentance, and "ungodly sorrow," which leads to death. In other words, guilt that is handled in the right way — that is admitted and dealt with — can be a corrective measure in a person's life, a catalyst spurring the guilty person on to greater strength and achievement. But guilt that is left unattended will fester like a splinter left in a finger and cause all kinds of problems. It is also likely to be the root of all sorts of aberrational behaviour — behaviour that begins as an attempt to hide from guilt and the pain it causes.

That is why the fifth of our Twelve Steps is so important:

I will admit to God, myself, and
another human being, the exact nature
of my wrongs.

Those who take this step find that confession brings freedom and joy.

Recently, an acquaintance who is associate pastor of a large church on the east coast told of a man who came to his office one afternoon, desperate to talk to someone about a problem that was "eating away" at him. This young man — in his early thirties — had been in the community for only a few months but had already proven to be a dedicated and hard-working member of the church. He seemed to be one of those people who have it all together.

That's why my friend was so surprised when the young man admitted, with great pain in his voice, that he had embezzled several thousand dollars from his previous employer in another state. Because of his position with the company he had found it fairly easy to manipulate the books, and nobody had suspected a thing.

But *he* knew what he had done, and he was having a very difficult time trying to live with it. In fact, he *couldn't* live with it. The time had come for him to confess, even though it would mean the loss of his reputation and possibly a lengthy stay in jail, separated from his wife and two young children.

He had considered the alternative — continuing to struggle with the guilt that was consuming him — and jail seemed to be the better option

He had confessed his guilt to God on numerous occasions, but that wasn't enough. He knew that he had to confess to another human being, as well as to those he had wronged. He was enlisting his pastor's support as he underwent what was sure to be an unpleasant experience of confessing and then facing up to the consequences.

I would like to tell you that because he voluntarily turned himself in his former employer was quick to forgive him and that he got off with nothing more than a slap on the wrist. Not so. He wound up spending nearly a year in jail, and he is struggling now to repay the thousands of dollars he stole. Nevertheless, the young man has never felt so good about himself, so optimistic about the future, or so full of joy about life in general. For him, the consequences of confession were quite severe — but they were not nearly as painful nor as damaging as carrying around a two ton load of unconfessed guilt.

Is there something this big in your life that you need to confess? Probably not. But we've all been guilty of wrong doing from time to time. After all, we're only human and human beings make mistakes.

When we do make mistakes, confession to God, ourselves, and others is tremendously important.

Confession Brings Release

My friend John C. remembers how difficult it was for him when he reached this step. When Carl, his sponsor in Alcoholics Anonymous, challenged him to confess the wrongs in his life, John responded with some vague generalities. Carl would have none of that. He wanted specifics.

"I knew that I was a thief, and a drunk, and a womanizer. And Carl made me talk about each of these things specifically," he remembers. "We talked until 3 A.M., and I shared things with him that I had never told anyone." The next morning, John awoke feeling "so good. I'd never been so high or felt so good in my life."

In step four, we actually began the process of confessing to ourselves as we took inventory of our lives, sorting out all of those shadowy parts of our existence that we had tried to keep hidden for so long.

If you were totally fearless and honest as you developed that inventory, you found out some things about yourself and your attitudes that you never really knew before — or if you knew them, you did your best to keep them hidden.

Whatever you've done in you life, God knows all about it already. When you confess to Him, you're not telling Him anything that's going to make Him angry. He will be happy that you have not tried to hold back, and you will find peace in the love and forgiveness He offers you.

Once we have admitted to ourselves and to God the exact nature of wrongs, it's time for the hardest part: admitting those same shortcomings to another human being. This is especially difficult for those of us who have spent most of our lives building fences or wearing masks in an effort to keep other people out — or at the very least, to keep them from seeing what's really going on in our lives. Whether fences are built to keep other people out or to keep us in, their end result is isolation and loneliness. Only when those fences are torn down and we come fully into community with others can we find the happiness and peace we really desire.

Those of us who are Protestants could learn an important lesson about confession from our Roman Catholic friends. I'm not suggesting that Protestants should make confession an official sacrament, but I'm afraid we tend to go too far in the other direction and forget about confession altogether. There is a great deal to be said for the Catholic practice of confessing sins to another person. That's a good thing to do, spiritually and psychologically.

Remember what we said about repressed anger — how it can cause physical and psychological damage? That's what can happen with unconfessed sin as well. Confession is a means by which we can obtain release from our sins, and without that release our feelings of guilt and shame can build up to the point where we can hardly stand up under the heavy load.

Too often today, the Christian church has become a place where people try to hide reality from God, from themselves, and from each other. Someone once said that the church is not a museum for saints but a hospital for sinners.

If you don't belong to a church, I suggest that you do one of two things:

1. Go church shopping. Attend the various churches in your neighbourhood and make a commitment to the one that fits you best. Don't expect to find a perfect church because they don't exit. Instead, look for a place where you can use your gifts and talents for your personal spiritual growth and for the growth of that congregation.
2. Seek out someone you can trust, with whom you can have an open "confessing" relationship. Whatever you do, don't just sit there and think, "Well, I don't have anyone to confess to, so I guess he's not talking to me." Yes, I am talking to you, and you need to have someone to talk to. Modern psychology backs me up in this — the human soul has a strong need to confess to another human soul.

Whether or not you are in a church, look for someone you can confide in. It should be someone who has qualities that you admire, who has your confidence, and with whom you feel comfortable. In just a moment, I'll give further suggestions as to who this person might be, but first I want to tell you a little bit about what's going on at Rancho Capistrano Community Church.

Because there is such a need for each of us to be able to share openly with another human being, we have instituted a "forgiveness ministry" and it has revolutionized our life together.

We have established a way for the people of our church to confess their sins to others who will listen in a nonthreatening and nondemeaning way, for there is no sin that is outside the realm of God's love and grace. What happens to the person who is able to confess this way? The burden is taken off his shoulders, the sin is placed in the past where it belongs, and he or she is free to begin to move on into the future.

The one with whom you have a confessing relationship won't be a stranger or a near-stranger. If you spill innermost secrets to a stranger, you're likely to find yourself the subject of a gossip column in the next morning's paper. You need to confess to someone you know and are confident that you can trust. Those are the relationships we're seeking to establish in our church: safe relationships.

We have been doing things for only a short while, and I can already sense that there is a new freedom among us — a new openness, a new spirit of love, cooperation, and unity. Lives have been changed through the exhilaration that comes from being set free. That's what admitting your faults to another person will do for you.

Who Will Hear My Confession?

It could be that the idea of admitting your faults and weaknesses to another person doesn't seem all that difficult until you start thinking about who that person might be. Every time you start to settle on someone, you think of a reason why he or she is not the one. Perhaps you're not sure you can trust the person to keep things in confidence, or may be you just wouldn't be comfortable sharing your innermost secrets with him or her. For any of dozens of other reasons you may just be having a downright difficult time looking for someone to confide in. Be confident, however, that there is someone who would be a good candidate.

A Therapist

If your innermost secrets are such that you would not want to confess them to a friend, then professional therapy may be in order. Did I hear someone ask, "But isn't that expensive?" It can be. But it is more expensive to keep everything bottled up inside you. Professional therapy can be very helpful, and a good therapist knows that everything you tell him must be kept in the strictest confidence.

Most health insurance carriers will cover most of the expenses for professional therapy, but in the event that you don't have insurance coverage, many therapists will use a sliding scale or make an affordable pay schedule. Many therapists also conduct or know of low-cost group-therapy sessions. If you say you can't afford it, you are probably making excuses. It is painful to face these issues and it takes plenty of courage, but the results will be worth the effort.

It's important that you find a therapist with whom you feel comfortable. If you have a strong faith in God, you certainly don't want to be unburdening yourself to someone who professes to be an atheist or who is antagonistic toward spiritual things. A good therapist can be a tremendous help, and it's important to spend as much time and effort as it takes to find one.

An Ordained Minister

It's best if you can talk to one of the ministers of your own church, or at least of your own denomination, but that is not absolutely necessary. Many ministers and rabbis set aside some time for counselling, and appointments can be made through the church secretary.

In most instances, ministers, priests, and rabbis are professionals who are able to listen effectively and offer valuable advice and encouragement.

Step five is not a one-time thing, nor is the inventory in step four. It may not be necessary to invest weeks or months in regular visits to a minister or therapist, but on the other hand, that may be very helpful, especially if you are under constant attack by the shadows of your life. Once you have begun to share the secrets of your inner life with someone, I wholeheartedly recommend that you continue the process in one way or another. In other words, as difficulties pile up, as you fall short of what you want to be, and if those shadows you wanted to get rid of seem to be regaining strength, you will need to continue to admit to another human being "the exact nature" of the problem.

When it comes to sharing problems that may exist in a relationship between a husband and wife, I strongly recommend that a professional counsellor be chosen as your listening partner — not a friend or family member. The reason is that the marriage relationship requires tremendous loyalty and discretion. A husband's first sense of loyalty should be to his wife and vice versa. The Bible says that a man should love his wife as much as he loves his own body, and Jesus himself described a married couple as being one flesh.

Has your husband let you down in some way? Then talk to him about it. If you feel that you can't do that right now, talk to a trained minister or counsellors who can listen impartially. Has your wife injured you in some way? The last thing you should do is pour out all the sad details to your sister (or even worse, to a friend of the opposite sex). What I'm saying is that you're not being disloyal if you share marriage problems with a professional therapist or with your minister, but you may be accused of disloyalty, and you may run the risk of causing even greater problems, if you share some of your most intimate secrets with other members of the family or with friends. All I am really saying is be wise and use discretion.

A Friend

In some cases a friend is the best person to hear your innermost thoughts. Perhaps he or she goes to the same church you attend. It could be a co-worker, someone with whom you play bridge on a regular basis, a member of your bowling team, or someone who belongs to the same service or social organisation. It doesn't have to be a person who knows you well or someone with incredible wisdom, but it should be someone who is a good listener, someone you can trust, and someone who displays a caring attitude. In other words, you may find this friend just about anywhere. You won't find him if you stay at home, behind locked doors, praying, "God, please send me a friend." You'll have to reach out. The old adage is true: "To get a friend you have to be one."

I have one strong recommendation about this friend. He or she should be a member of your sex — especially if you are married. This is true for two reasons: "First, because a woman is better able to understand the problems that trouble a woman, and a man is better able to understand and support a man. Second, because as much as you might try to safeguard against it, there is bound to be a bit of sexual "mystery" in any close relationship between members of the opposite sex, and when you're talking about the intimate level of sharing that we're discussing, that "mystery" could lead from friendship to romance.

Please understand that I'm not one of those who think it is impossible for men and women to be good friends and nothing more than friends, but I am also perceptive enough to realise that such friendships can and often do lead to intimate involvement. I have counselled people who told me that the last thing they ever thought would happen to them was that they would become involved in an extramarital affair. But a friendship with a member of the opposite sex took a wrong turn somewhere, and that's exactly what happened.

Confessing When You Haven't Done Anything Wrong

Not too long ago I had the privilege of meeting Marilyn Van Derbur Atler, a beautiful, gracious woman. She is a former Miss America, an elegant woman who has always been in great demand as a motivational speaker. In fact, she is one of the very few women who have been invited to speak to the executives and other employees of huge corporations such as Xerox and IBM. If you have ever had the opportunity to hear her speak, you know why. She is a fabulous speaker, one who is able to make you believe that you have the power within you to do great things and is able to give you the desire and determination to do them.

Well, in spite of her elegance, her beauty, and her grace; in spite of the fact that she is so good when it comes to getting others to believe in themselves, Mrs. Atler carried around for years a deep, dark, and very painful secret.

When she was a young girl, she was molested by her father. This was not a one-time thing, which would be bad enough, but a molestation that continued on a regular basis for some time. Night after night after night her father would come to her room and force his little girl to engage in sexual acts with him.

And Marilyn never told a soul.

As you can imagine, there was tremendous damage being done to the mind and soul of this beautiful little girl. What that damage eventually did was to effectually split her personality in two. For all practical purposes, she was two different people living in the same body. She was the daytime Marilyn — intelligent, outgoing, popular — and she was the nighttime Marilyn — withdrawn, frightened, spending much of the night curled up in the fetal position.

During the day, she was her school's student body president. She was active in numerous organisations. She was a consistent beauty pageant winner. She never brought home a report card that wasn't covered with As. At night, she lay curled up in fear, waiting and hoping this would be the night when she would be left alone.

Finally, the molestation stopped. Marilyn grew into a young woman. She went out into the world and made a tremendous success of her life as Miss America, as a businesswoman, and as a motivational speaker. She was a wife and mother and she was happy with her life. The daytime Marilyn seemed to have won the battle, and the nighttime Marilyn was pushed into the background and forgotten. Not only was she forgotten, but all of the sordid details of her father's abuse were forgotten as well. This had become one of the buried shadows of Marilyn's life. Because it was never dealt with, it was a shadow with the potential of causing her continued harm. That's the way things stayed for more than twenty years. From time to time she caught a glimpse of something from those old days, but she didn't know what it was; and sometimes she felt depressed in spite of herself, but she didn't know why.

Then one day when she looked at her own daughter, something happened deep within her. A light was coming on and she was beginning to see that long-lost nighttime Marilyn. She wasn't really gone. She was hidden away in a closet, but she still existed.

At that time, her daughter was about the age Marilyn was when her father's sexual abuse began. When Marilyn saw her little girl in a special way that day, she began to remember the flashes of pain and unhappiness from her own childhood. She became depressed and angry until she couldn't function at all. She couldn't get out of bed, go to work, or participate in any other ordinary functions of daily life. Her depression was so severe that all she could do was lie in bed and cry. Deep down in her subconscious, Marilyn knew what had happened to her as a child, but she couldn't bring herself to face the awful truth. Her subconscious would not "confess" to her rational mind those things that had happened so long ago. Because Marilyn Van Derbur Atler is a very brave woman, she would not let things rest until she dealt with that shadow. As she struggled to remember the events of long ago, everything began to come clear.

What was happening was that Marilyn was confessing to her self some of the events she had tried to repress for so long. In doing that she was taking a tremendously important step in the journey toward spiritual healing. Since then, she has "confessed" to the public also, hoping to help other girls and women who have experienced the same sort of trauma. She has written a book; she has made numerous public appearances; and she has appeared on several television shows, talking about what happened to her as a child and her struggle to recognise and unite the two disparate personalities that fought for control of her being.

As she has done all of these things, Marilyn has grown stronger and healthier, and she can tell you now that she is finally finding peace.

You see, confession doesn't necessarily mean that the person confessing has done something wrong. Marilyn certainly didn't do anything wrong, although like many innocent victims of incest, she may have felt some guilt for what was happening to her. (Isn't it terrible that a little girl who was victimised by her father would have to carry the added burden of feeling guilty for what he had done?)

Confession can be an admission of guilt, but in this case it is a baring of the soul, an admission of the way things really are or were. It is a clearing of the air that helps to bring release and freedom.

The Confession Session

Once you have become aware of the need to confess to God, yourself, and another human being the exact nature of your problem, and once you have found the person with whom you want to share, there are a few guidelines you should follow:

- Find a place where you can talk without interruptions or distractions.
- Give yourself all the time you need. Don't try to sandwich a confession session between other pressing appointments. It's too important for that. If one time together isn't enough, then schedule other times.
- Remember that all you are doing in step five is admitting the exact nature of your wrongs. The purpose is not to get advice from the other person nor to tell him what you plan to do to fix those areas of your life.
- Always remember that confidentiality must be observed. You should expect the person who is listening to you to keep everything you have told him to himself, and you should be prepared

to do the same for him. Whatever is said between the two of you does not go out of the room.

- Do your best to avoid getting sidetracked. Stay focused on the task at hand. Because some of the issues you need to talk about may be especially sensitive, or even embarrassing, it's easy to avoid them by spending your time together engaging in small talk, which helps to ease the tension but doesn't accomplish the purpose for your getting together.
- It's a good idea to pray with each other before and after your time together. Before the session you can ask God to bless the time and enable you to say the things that need to be said. Ask for clarity of mind and the ability to be totally honest. Afterwards thank him for allowing you to do what you've done; pray that what has been said may be kept in confidence and that you and your listener may both be strengthened and encouraged by what has taken place.

Remember that you must be as open and honest as you can possibly be. If you can truthfully say that you have not only been honest but as thorough as you know how to be, then you're ready to begin the process of eliminating all those problem areas from your life.

6

Getting Ready to Deal with the Ghosts That Haunt You

We've spent a lot of time in this book talking about total honesty — and there's no need to stop now.

So let me ask you a question. Is there some "sin" in your life that you really enjoy and don't want to get rid of? If you're a normal, everyday variety human being, and if you're answering with total honesty, I'd be willing to bet the answer is yes.

Now notice that I put the word *sin* in quotation marks. I did that because the sort of thing I'm referring to may not really be much of a sin at all. It might just be something that you know you shouldn't do — for whatever reason — but you enjoy it so much it's hard to envision your life without it. Or it may be something "big," like addiction to drugs or alcohol, a seeming inability to tell the truth, or overwhelming sexual desires that threaten your marriage — and perhaps even your life. Whatever it is, you'd like to pray, "Dear God, please eliminate this thing from my life," but on the other hand, you're afraid to pray that prayer because he might do it!

You may want to change, and then, at the same time, you don't. Not until John C. really wanted to change did anything happen in his life. There are many different types of sin and behaviour that people want to hang on to. Some people hold tight to:

- Anger and resentment
- Martyrdom
- Illicit sexual behaviour
- Addiction to drugs or alcohol
- Abusive relationships

The list could go on and on. Name a wrong attitude or dysfunctional behaviour and chances are very good that someone somewhere is holding on to it with all his might. He might say he wants to let go, but that's not true.

At step six of our Twelve-Step program, we want to reach the point where we can pray, "Lord, take this away from me," and honestly mean it. Step six says:

I will make myself entirely ready to have God remove any defects from my character and bring about the necessary changes in my life.

Let's take just a few moments to recap where we've been and see how the previous five steps have brought us to this point. The first thing we did was to admit that we were powerless to overcome the difficulties facing us and that our lives were unmanageable. That rather hopeless thought was quickly followed up by an acknowledgment that God is greater than we are and that He is able to bring restoration. The third step was to turn our lives over to God, realising that this is the only way to appropriate His power for our lives. Step four took us through the painful process of making a "searching and fearless" moral inventory of our lives, and in step five we used that inventory to "admit to God, ourselves, and another human being the exact nature of our wrongs."

Look how far we've come already! When we started out on this journey we were powerless. Now we have the power of God in our lives. When we began, we may have known that things weren't quite right. We knew about some specific problem areas in our lives, but we didn't have a handle on the root causes of those problems, nor did we have an overall view of the things that needed to be changed.

It's simple truth that you can't fix something unless you know it's broken. Because of that, the person who knows what's broken has an advantage over the person who doesn't. We now know what needs to be fixed (or most of what needs to be fixed), and that is a big step.

Finally, when we set out on this road to spiritual healing, many of us were isolated, left to face the difficulties of life all by ourselves. Now, by sharing those shadows in our lives with others, we have enlisted their support and encouragement. They have become our allies in the battle to achieve spiritual maturity.

None of us have yet arrived. We still have quite a ways to go, but when we are able to look back and see how far we've already come, it gives us strength for the rest of the journey.

Isn't it good to know, too, that even though the path ahead may be steep and difficult, it's not a path you have to walk by yourself? God is with you, and He promises:

> He gives strength to the weary
>   and increases the power of the weak.
> Even youths grow tired and weary,
>   and young men stumble and fall;
> but those who hope in the Lord
>   will renew their strength.
> They will soar on wings like eagles;
>   they will run and not grow weary,
>   they will walk and not be faint.
>
> [Isa.40:29-31]

In his letter to the church at Rome, the apostle Paul asks a rhetorical question: "If God is for us, who can be against us?" The answer to that question is that it really doesn't matter who or what may be against you. If God is on your side (and He is!) all the forces of hell may be coming against you, and you'll still be able to emerge victoriously.

There's a little saying I've heard from time to time that I really like: "Help me remember, Lord, that nothing is going to happen today that you and I can't handle together." It's like my father's prayer. "Oh, Lord, you have a plan for my life today. I want to be a part of it."

It wouldn't be a bad idea to buy a plaque with that message on it and put it someplace where you'll see it every day — a constant reminder that whatever battle you're facing, you have an awesomely powerful ally!

On her desk in our house, Donna keeps a devotional calendar and a couple of devotional books. Every day, as she turns the page on her calendar, she reads a Bible verse, which reminds her of God's love and power. She also reads the meditation for the day from at least one of her devotional books, and sometimes from both of them. There are other devotional or inspirational calendars in other areas of the house.

I think that's a great idea. Just about everyone keeps a calendar or two, so why not have one that's going to remind you of God's love and care for you every time you use it? That's one way you can become more aware of God's presence, and you will be benefited as you go through the day.

Step six isn't as much something you do as it is an attitude you take on. I'm not talking about making yourself "good enough" to ask God to remove those defects from your life. I'm not suggesting that you fast to purify your system, that you spend a year or two living by yourself on some distant mountain to strengthen your soul, or anything like that. You don't have to be "good enough" to ask God to do something for you. The fact is that you could never in a million years do anything to make yourself worthy of God's grace. No matter, He stands ready to help you anyway.

Step six means that you change your attitude so that you are willing to have God remove certain responses to shadows that have been part of your life for so many years. In fact, you must not only be willing, but anxious.

Like my wife, who uses devotional desk calendars and the like to remind her every day of God's love and power, you will probably need to reinforce on a daily basis the attitude of wanting God to remove those shadows from your life. It's hard to give up an attitude or a behaviour that's been a part of you for so long — especially when that attitude or behaviour has been part of your defence system. Once you've made the decision that this is what you want, you have to stick with it. Sticking with it may mean recommitting yourself to that decision on a daily or even hourly basis — however often you are tempted to fall back into your old lifestyle.

It would be great, wouldn't it, if God would just send out some sort of supernatural bolt from the blue and in an instant completely remake your character. If you're old enough, you may remember when Ajax laundry detergent had a television commercial that featured the White Knight. He would come charging up on his shiny white horse and zap anyone who was dirty. A woman is waiting at a bus stop on a rainy day when a careless driver comes by and splashes mud all over her. The lady has somewhere important to go, but now she's covered with mud! What's she going to do? Never fear. Here comes the White Knight from Ajax. Zap! He points his lance at her and she's as clean and fresh as can be!

Those were effective commercials, and I'm sure they sold a lot of soap. That's not the way Ajax really works, and it's certainly not the way God works. He is willing and able to help you remove all of those troubling areas from your life, but He wants you to be involved in the process. He wants you to grow and become stronger, and He'll help you to do that. He'll even guide you through the process if you are willing to have Him do that.

At the same time, it's pretty much true that "no pain means no gain." It may take some time for you to get to the point where you are honestly ready to see any and all character defects removed from your life, and that's why I say that you'll have to approach the situation with earnestness.

It is true that I have seen men and women instantly transformed by God's power. I have seen men who were consumed with anger and hatred become instantly loving and open when they were confronted by the living God. I have seen people who seemed to be hopelessly addicted to drugs and alcohol set free in an instant. You remember how I told you about the way God instantaneously changed me. One moment I was nearly overcome by fear at the thought of standing before a large group and giving a speech, and the next instant I was enjoying it. So, yes, that sort of thing can and does happen, but such events are exceptions to the rule, and to count on something like that is not wise. The rule is that God doesn't want to do this thing for you — He wants to do it with you!

Four Things to Remember

As you strive to get to the point where you really are willing to have God help you get rid of all the character defects in your life — no matter how comfortable those defects might feel to you or how much you may have depended on them to protect you in life's rougher moments — you need to keep at least four things in mind.

Be Patient

These character traits and behaviours you want to eliminate may be very deeply ingrained in your personality. That means you have to be patient with yourself and with God. Don't give up, don't quit trying to get to the point where you're willing to let go of things like anger or a tendency to isolate yourself. Seek to have the attitude illustrated by the apostle Paul:

> Not that I have already obtained all this, or have already been made perfect, but I press on to take hold of that for which God took hold of me. Forgetting what is behind and straining toward what is ahead, I press on toward the goal to win the prize for which God has called me heavenward in Christ Jesus.
>
> [Paul. 3:12-14]

That's the attitude you have to have. Forget about what's happened in the past. Forget about all the times you've failed (or think you've failed). Concentrate on the present, on what lies ahead, and press on toward the goal. Are you realising that in spite of everything you've tried to do, you still have an urge to hang on to something that should be let go? Keep on working on your attitude and trusting God to help you, and eventually you'll find that your desires truly are changing.

A few years ago, Donna and I changed our eating habits. We quit eating things like butter, cheese, creamy sauces, ice cream — we eliminated fatty foods from our diets. At first, it wasn't easy. It was especially difficult to eat a baked potato that wasn't loaded with butter and sour cream. As time has gone by, however, our tastes have changed. Today, I couldn't even think about eating a baked potato that was swimming in butter. The very idea is totally unappealing and unappetising. Our tastes have changed in other ways, too. For example, we used to drink low-fat milk, but now we've switched to non-fat, and we find that we actually prefer the taste. What has happened is that our desires have changed to the point where we would rather eat the things that are best for us, and we are healthier and feel better as a result. Our desires changed over time, and so can yours.

Stay Positive

Welcome small beginnings. There's an old peanuts cartoon in which Charlie Brown is talking about glaciers. In his own succinct way, he says that glaciers sometimes follow an erratic path. A glacier will move a foot forward, and then melting will cause it to move a couple of feet backward. That's the way it goes: a foot forward here, two feet backward there, another couple of feet forward, and so on. "Which," Charlie says, "reminds me a lot of myself."

Do you tend to see yourself as a glacier? Instead of moving steadily ahead, do you seem to move in an erratic pattern — forward here, backward there? You may have taken one small positive step forward but followed it with two big negative steps backward. In that case, concentrate on the one small positive instead of those two large negative. In other words, look for positive signs that you are moving in the right direction. Don't give in to nagging doubt, that negative voice that picks on you and tells you you'll never get to where you want to be. You took one step forward, and that's great. You can take another one and another one, on and on until you're virtually running in the right direction. Positive! Forward! That's the name of this game! So concentrate on the plus side of things, and you will soon find that the positive movement far outweighs the negative.

Communicate with God

It's important that you talk to God on a daily basis. Ask for His help. Tell Him what's on your mind. He's there for you, and He will listen.

If you had a chance to sit down with the president of the United States, tell him what was on your mind, and ask for his help in a certain matter, wouldn't you do it? I'm sure most of us would. You have an opportunity to sit down with the King of the entire universe, tell Him what's on your mind, and ask for His help. It would be a tragic mistake not to take advantage of that opportunity.

But let me say something about the way you talk to Him. Do it in humility, admitting your own shortcomings, and with a hopeful attitude about the future. Pray this prayer. "Thank you, Lord, for yesterday. Thank you for today. Help me to pray this prayer again tomorrow."

Unfortunately, some people seem to have the idea that God is sitting around, just waiting for our orders like some cosmic vending machine. Of course, that's not at all the way it is. After all, He is God! Nobody orders God around! When we ask humbly, God will give us what we need. But only when we need it, and when we can handle it.

Be Aware of Your Feelings

You should always try to be aware of your motives and your emotions. Strive to face issues as they come up in your life. Don't turn away from them. I say this, first of all, because some people have a tendency to exchange one destructive behaviour for another. For example, the person who gives up smoking may begin overeating. He feels good because he's "kicked the habit," but he's really just exchanged one vice for another. He has found another area on which he can concentrate his attention and thus avoid looking at life's more difficult issues. If he were totally honest and in touch with his feelings, he would have to admit that his addictive behaviour had not really changed; only the focus of that behaviour had changed. It's good to question your motives, to be sure that you are not still covering up and refusing to confront the real issues of life.

When they are dealing with a recovering alcoholic, many therapists wait until there have been twelve to eighteen months of sobriety before they start working on the serious issues within that person's life. It may take that long for the alcoholic to get to the point where he can face up to, much less deal with, those larger issues.

As you modify your lifestyle, you are almost certainly going to be confronted by some difficult and painful issues. It's perfectly all right to admit to your pain — but face up to it. Don't turn away or seek to hide from it. Being aware of your feelings — and knowing that it's all right to feel the way you do — can be a big step on the road to recovery.

Scripture Will Encourage You

What else can help you get to the point of being entirely ready to have God remove any character defects from your life? I suggest that you spend time reading and meditating on Scripture verses that will remind you of God's grace, patience, and faithfulness.

> This is the confidence we have in approaching God: that if we ask anything according to His will, He hears us. And if we know that He hears us — whatever we ask — we know that we have what we asked of Him.
>
> [1 John 5: 14-15]

There are literally hundreds of encouraging verses like these in the Bible. Read them, let them sink in, and then you'll be better able to trust God totally with your life. It's important that you understand and believe completely that God is able and willing to hear and help you and that the plan He has devised for you is much better than anything you could possibly have devised for yourself. It is, you know.

So, are you ready to move on, to ask God to remove any and all defects from your character? If so, it's time for step seven.

7

Okay, Lord, It's All Yours!

On a trip to the United States, the Pope was very late for an appointment, so he told the driver of his limousine to drive as fast as he possibly could.

The driver tried but he couldn't drive fast enough for the Pope, who finally said in exasperation, "Just pull over, and I'll drive."

So, with the regular driver in the back seat and the Pope at the wheel, the limo went flying through town. His holiness was really putting "the pedal to the metal." Not only was he zipping along at close to eighty miles an hour, but he was also running red lights and breaking just about every traffic law there is.

Well, not even the Pope is going to get away with that for very long. And sure enough, it was only a matter of time before a highway patrol car was right behind that limo, with its siren wailing and its blue lights flashing. After the limo pulled over, one of the patrolmen waited in the car while his partner went up to issue the citation. A few minutes later he came back, and his partner knew that he hadn't been gone long enough to write out a ticket.

"Didn't you give him a ticket?"

"Nope."

"Why not?"

"I was afraid to. He's too important!"

"Too important? Who is it? Al Gore?"

"More important than that!"

"Bill Clinton?"

"More important than that!"

"More important than the president of the United States? Well, who in the world is it?"

"I'm not sure — but the Pope is driving him!"

Okay, so maybe it didn't really happen. My point in telling this story is to ask you a very important question: Who is driving your life? You can have a driver who's more important than Al Gore or Bill Clinton or the Pope or Billy Graham or anybody else you can think of. God wants to be in the driver's seat of your life.

In fact, He's just waiting for you to get out of the way so He can take the wheel! That's precisely what step seven is all about:

I will humbly ask God to remove my shortcomings.

Way back in step three, you made a decision to turn your life over to God. I said at that time that surrendering your life to Him was not a once-for-all-time experience. It's something that must be done again and again, for two reasons:

- We have a tendency to try to take back parts of our lives from God's control. "I didn't really mean to give you this part of my life. I think I'll just take this back, and this, and may be a little bit of this over there."
- A complete surrender to God is often a gradual process. Conversion may happen in an instant, but complete surrender rarely does. Only as you walk with God on a daily basis, getting to know Him better and better, are you likely to surrender completely to His will.

Because of all this, it's good to occasionally review problem areas of your life and recommit to Him.

I heard a story about a great violinist who came to Houston to give a concert. This violinist had recently spent thousands of dollars to purchase a Stradivarius violin. Naturally, there was a great deal of interest in this exquisite instrument, and all the news media carried stories about this wonderful opportunity to hear the fabulous music that such a violin would produce.

The local newspapers ran photographs of the Stradivarius and published articles telling about its history and the marvellous tonal quality of the instrument. On and on it went. There were a few words spoken about the violinist himself, but not very many. Most of the praise went to the violin.

When the night of the concert came, the hall was packed, and the audience was not disappointed. The crowd was thrilled with every note, and the auditorium was filled with wave after wave of tremendous applause. When the concert ended, the appreciation of the audience was demonstrated by a prolonged standing ovation.

Then the violinist did something quite shocking. He took his violin, that beautiful instrument that had been the source of such wonderful music all night long, and lifted it over his head. After the crowd rose to its feet in adulation, he brought the instrument down — hard — across his knee. Its back was broken, the strings hung loose, and it was completely worthless.

As you can imagine, a gasp of horror swept through the auditorium. People wondered if the violinist had completely lost his mind. He raised his hand to quiet the murmuring and told them, "This is not my Stradivarius. I went down to the pawn shop and bought this violin for ninety-five dollars."

You see, it wasn't so much the quality of the instrument that produced those beautiful, soul-stirring sounds. It was the quality of the person playing that instrument.

Some of us may be feeling at this point in our lives like the ninety-five-dollar pawn shop violin, living in a world full of Stradivariuses. After all, we've gone through six steps where we've examined our lives in minute detail, looking over our personal histories and finding all of the negativity and character defects in our lives. I'm sure it would be safe to say that most of us haven't really cared too much for most of what we've seen. Then we look around at what other people are doing with their lives, and we think things like, "Boy, if only I had his talent," or "If only I had her money," or "I sure wish I were as smart as she is."

The reality is that it doesn't matter if you're not as smart or rich or clever or beautiful as some other person. If your life is held in God's hands, then you, too, can produce the most beautiful music imaginable. The key is to get your focus away from yourself and on to the Great Musician — God Himself.

That's what we're aiming for in step seven. In this step we take the focus off ourselves and place it on the Creator. We shift our attention away from the violin and put it on the one who creates the music. It enables us to avert our eyes from our own weakness and fasten them on God's strength.

Accomplishing Great Things

There are many accounts in the Bible of ordinary men and women who accomplished great things simply because they let God have control of their lives. Right now, I want to briefly consider three of these people: Moses, Gideon, and David.

Moses

Moses was eighty years old when God called him to lead the children of Israel out of their captivity in Egypt. He hadn't really done anything spectacular with his life and there wasn't much reason to think he was going to start then. Besides all of that, he had a speech impediment.

When God told Moses that he had been chosen to rescue the Israelites, his immediate reaction was "Who am I, that I should go to Pharaoh and bring the

Israelites out of Egypt?" And when God insisted, Moses protested further. "O, Lord I have never been eloquent, neither in the past nor since you have spoken to your servant. I am slow of speech and tongue".

Despite all of his initial protests, Moses finally surrendered his will to God and became the first great leader of the Israelite nation — one of the greatest men who ever lived. It wasn't that Moses was someone with such special abilities. He was just someone who was willing to let himself be used by God.

Gideon

During Gideon's day, the nation of Israel was occupied by the vicious Midianites. The Midianites were great warriors and so brutal that many of the Israelites hid out from them by living in caves in the mountains.

One day, an angel appeared to a young man named Gideon and told him that he had been chosen to lead the Israelites in a fight to reclaim their independence. Young Gideon reacted the way you might expect him to act. First of all, he figured the Israelites were so weak and the Midianites so strong that any sort of rebellion would probably be crushed fairly easily. And then, he thought the same thing Moses had thought: "Who am I?" "But Lord," he said, "how can I save Israel? My clan is the weakest in Manasseh, and I am the least in my family".

Guess what happened. Gideon trusted God and led the rebellion, just as God had told him to do, and the mighty Midianites were driven from the land. Gideon was just a young man — a farmer, really — but in God's hands he became a mighty warrior and the means through which his people regained their freedom.

David

King David was the greatest king the nation of Israel ever had. And yet, you may remember what happened when the prophet Samuel went to David's house to anoint him king.

All Samuel knew was that the Lord had sent him to the house of a man named Jesse and that one of Jesse's sons was to be anointed as the new king of Israel. Jesse brought all of his tall, strong, handsome sons before Samuel. One by one, seven young men passed before the prophet, and each time Samuel said, "This is not the one the Lord has chosen."

After all seven had been rejected, the prophet asked, "Are these all the sons you have?"

"Well," came the reply, "there's still the youngest, but he's out taking care of the sheep."

The implication was that this youngest couldn't possibly be the one the Lord had chosen. He was just a boy, weak and small next to his older brothers. But Samuel insisted, so Jesse summoned his youngest son from the fields. When Samuel saw the young man, he knew beyond any doubt that this was the one God had chosen as king. There in the presence of his father and his brothers, he anointed the youth, who went on to be the greatest king in all of Israel's history — the one through whose line Jesus would come.

Others God Used

There are many other accounts in the Scriptures of God bringing greatness out of people whom others considered incapable of greatness — or who did not consider themselves capable of great things.

When Saul was chosen as the first king of Israel, he was so insecure that he hid to keep Samuel from anointing him.

Mary, the mother of Jesus, was a mere girl of perhaps fourteen when the angel Gabriel told her she was going to give birth to the Messiah. She had a difficult time believing that she had been chosen for such a tremendous blessing — and certainly those who knew Mary and Joseph wouldn't have put the couple on their list of "most likely to be chosen by God to be the parents of the Anointed One." But they were.

A Common Denominator: Humility

The thread that runs through the lives of all of these people is humility. None of them accomplished anything on their own. They all responded rather reluctantly to God's call to greatness, but they did respond, and they all accomplished great things.

I believe that in one way or another God is calling all of His people to great things. I know beyond any doubt that He can accomplish great things through anyone who is committed to doing his will. I'm not saying that you'll become a king or a queen, or even that the world will notice what you do; many great things are done quietly behind the scenes. Perhaps the great things you will do will consist of overcoming the shadows of your life and fulfilling all the potential God built into you, potential that has, until now, remained unfulfilled because of something that happened to you when you were younger, some shadow that's troubled you for years and years.

In his book, *Mere Christianity,* C.S. Lewis has some excellent thoughts about what it will be like when we have all passed into the afterlife. Only then, he suggests, will we know what people have done with what they were given.

God doesn't look at outward appearances but at what's in the heart. He doesn't care as much about what you've done as He does about what you've done with what you were given to work with. I am convinced that when we get there, we will find that some of the greatest heroes in heaven are folks who never even got their names in the local newspaper while they were living here on earth. The world didn't take note of what they did because they did it quietly, behind the scenes. But God noticed, and He will see that appropriate recognition is given. It may not happen in this life, but it will happen.

One at a Time

Before I go on, I want you to understand that I don't doubt the power of God to do anything — not for one minute. I believe with my whole heart that He created everything we see around us, including you and me. Having said that, I also know that it is often true that prayer works more like a medicine than like radical surgery.

What do I mean by that? Suppose you were sick; so you went to the doctor and he prescribed an antibiotic and told you to take two tablespoons twice daily for ten days. Would it do you any good to drink the entire bottle of medicine immediately on leaving the doctor's office? Of course not! In fact, doing something like that would only add to your miseries.

It's the same with prayer. It often takes continued prayer, over a period of many days, or even years, to bring about the answers we seek. Why is this true? The only thing that grows fast in my garden are the weeds. The flowers take time to blossom. Based on my own life and on things other people have told me, this is most often the way life is, too.

In May of 1983, a member of my church, Laura Jean Taylor, was told by her doctor that she had ovarian cancer. Later, he disclosed that she had only eighteen months to live. We put Laura Jean on our prayer list and have been praying for her ever since. Today she still has cancer, but she is alive and happy and has brought life to many people in our congregation. God has not chosen to remove her cancer but to use it to encourage many people. He has extended her life nearly *ten times* longer than her doctor predicted.

I'm telling you about Laura Jean because I don't want you to become discouraged and give up if it seems that there is no immediate bolt of lightning in response to your prayer requests. Going back to the analogy of the antibiotic — suppose that the doctor had given you a bottle of medicine and told you to take it for ten days, but after the fourth or fifth day you weren't feeling very much better so you decided to just give up? Perhaps in another day or two you would have been feeling just fine, but you gave up too early.

Another scenario could be that in four or five days you felt so much better that you decided you didn't need the medicine any more. Do you know what would happen then? More than likely, the illness would come right back and you'd have to go back to the doctor for another prescription. Like many of the other things I'm telling you, I know all about this from personal experience!

My point is that in order to become the person you want to be, you're going to need to pray, pray, and pray some more. Don't give up because nothing seems to be happening — you might be poised on the edge of victory. At the same time, don't quit praying about something until you are absolutely sure God has given you the victory. Some of the things we're talking about may be so deeply ingrained in your character that they'll need to be included in your prayers for the rest of your life. That's fine. It's not a sign of weakness — yours or God's!

Strive to pray in this fashion: "Oh, Lord, you have a plan for my life today. I want to be part of it." The idea is to move one step at a time, one day at a time, committing each one to God as it unfolds and recognising His mercies and benefits in each.

There's another way that prayer is like medicine. Back in the 19th century, there used to be men who would go around the country selling "tonic" in what were known as "medicine shows." And what a tonic it was! A few swallows of the elixir they sold could cure any disease known to man, and a few that weren't. Not really, of course, but that's the sort of claims that were made by these medicine men.

The reality is that there is no super drug that will cure all of your ills at once. If you go to the doctor because you have a sore throat, an earache, and an upset stomach, he'll probably wind up prescribing three different medicines, one for each of your problems.

When it comes to prayer, it's trying to take the easy way out when we say, "Okay, God, here's a list of all my problems. Now please fix everything."

Experience tells me that it works better if you specialise. You have your inventory of the behaviours you want to change. Use that to take those various behaviours before the Lord one at a time. I suggest that you start out with the ones that cause the most damage in your life.

Suppose you take mind-altering drugs — alcohol, narcotics, or over-the-counter drugs like diet pills, sleeping pills, or caffeine tablets. You've struggled against this addiction for so long that you've begun to think there is no way you'll ever be set free. This should be the first thing that you talk to God about.

You may not have a problem with drugs, but whatever it is that causes you the most difficulty and pain, go on the offensive against it with daily, continual prayer. Seek to back up your prayers with actions. In other words, ask God for the strength to overcome this particular problem, and then follow through by seeking to take appropriate steps as He gives you that strength.

Just start there, and then as you gain ground in that area, you can begin to pray about the other areas as well. Be sure to spend lots of concentrated time in prayer on each of the areas you want to change. Remember, "Do not be anxious about anything, but in everything, by prayer and petition, with thanksgiving, present your requests to God".

It's Okay to Feel Bad

You may be surprised to find that, even though you are moving full speed ahead in the direction you want to travel, you feel slightly insecure, or even strangely sad.

Have you ever known anyone who was trying to quit smoking? I have, and that person isn't always the most pleasant to be around. Usually, it's just the opposite. He may be extremely cranky and irritable. He knows he needs to stop smoking; he's proud of what he's doing; but he'd just about give his right arm if someone would hand him a lit cigarette and say, "I just heard on the news that the surgeon general now says these things are *good* for you!"

You have depended on your behaviour patterns to do something for you just as the smoker has always depended on his cigarette to relax him. The process of getting rid of those patterns won't always find you jumping up and down with joy. Remember, these addictive behaviours may have been used to help you survive some very difficult situations in the past. They helped you so that you didn't have to deal with painful issues before you were ready to deal with them. Now that the time has come to deal with the issues, however, the behaviour patterns are harmful because they stand in the way.

Now, the smoker is dying for a cigarette, but after several months without smoking, he'll probably say, "I've never felt better in my life! I have so much energy, I don't cough and wheeze all the time, and I don't burn holes in my clothes anymore!"

My intention is not to pick on smokers — although if you smoke, you ought to quit — but it is to show that it's okay to feel bad while you're working on overcoming an ingrained behaviour pattern. Don't worry, the joy will come! In most cases you will probably feel worse before you begin to feel better. In cases where there has been chemical abuse and addiction to alcohol, nicotine, or other drug, withdrawal can cause severe physical changes. In these severe cases, medical attention is advised. In cases of emotional addiction, there is likely to be extreme anxiety when people, things, or behaviours that were destructive are removed and painful issues and memories are dealt with for the first time. Again, professional help is advised. Since the destructive habit has been let go, the person has no other choice than to face the issues that caused him to escape into destructive behaviour in the first place. So don't see a bad feeling as a sign of defeat. It may very well be a sign of progress.

The important thing to remember is that it is precisely when you are feeling your worst that you need to hold on to God and his promises the tightest. There are wonderful promises in the Psalms to remind you that God is with you in times of trouble and will keep you safe and secure, even though you may feel lousy.

> Good and upright is the Lord;
> therefore he instructs sinners in his ways.
> He guides the humble in what is right
> and teaches them his way.
> All the ways of the Lord are loving and faithful
> for those who keep the demands of his covenant.
> For the sake of of your name O Lord;
> forgive my iniquity, though it is great.
>
> [Ps.25:8-11]

If You Can't Eliminate It, Use It

Before we move on to step eight, I want to remind you once again that not all of the shadows in your life need to be completely eliminated. In some cases, however, it may be necessary to modify them and learn to use them in a positive and beneficial way.

For example, it is not a bad thing to realise that you are the type who wants to avoid confrontation and that you have a tendency to be the peacemaker, but you must learn to stand up for yourself and have intact emotional and spiritual boundaries. You must also learn to confront in appropriate and constructive ways. Remember that "confrontation done with empathy is an act of grace; confrontation done without empathy is a graceless act."

There's no need to completely eliminate from your personality the tendency to avoid conflict, but you'll need to modify it so that it's helpful and not harmful. Carried to its extreme, this tendency turns you into a doormat. Used to its best advantage, it earns you a reputation as a skilled diplomat. Jesus himself said that peacemakers would be called the children of God.

Before we move on, I want to leave you with this prayer, from the Big Book of Alcoholics Anonymous:

> My Creator, I am now willing that you should have all of me, good and bad. I pray that you now remove from me every single defect of character which stands in the way of my usefulness to you and my fellows. Grant me the strength, as I go out from here, to do your bidding. Amen.

Coming up next: It's time to make amends!

8

Getting Ready to Say "I'm Sorry"

This is going to be tough. But then you already knew that. After all, almost every one of the seven steps we've taken up until now has been difficult, so why should step eight be the exception?

Actually, step eight is when you turn the corner and begin to take responsibility for your own actions. No fair blaming your mom or dad or brother or sister or teacher or preacher any longer. It's true that these people may have done some things to you that caused you to respond in certain unhealthy ways. As a result, you may have caused harm to others.

Step eight is:

I will make a list of all the people I have harmed by my past behaviour and become willing to make amends.

This step involves only getting to the place of being willing to make amends. Then step nine will involve actually making amends. I don't want to get ahead of myself here, but I thought you needed to know that step eight does not include actually making the amends. In this step, we are compiling the list of things we need to set right and we are developing a willing heart. Don't take step eight lightly, however, because it is essential preparation for what comes next. It's not easy to be honest and make the list, and it's even more difficult to create a heart that's willing to talk to people you have harmed or offended. Remember, I'm talking about specific things that you did that you know were wrong, for which you need to offer specific and honest apologies.

Make a List and Check It Twice

The first order of business is figuring out who it is that you need to make amends to and why. In order to make these determinations, it might be helpful to go back to the inventory you prepared in step four. As you review that list, and see the personality characteristics you decided to change, think about ways those characteristics may have caused you to harm people. As much as is possible, think about specific situations and write down the names of specific people who were harmed by your actions.

Human nature being what it is, most people usually go overboard when it comes to excusing themselves for their behaviour. For step eight, we want to go overboard in the other direction, and refuse to even consider the fact that there might have been mitigating circumstances for our actions. Do your best to think of everyone who might be due an apology from you.

What you are doing here is for your good. It is not really for the benefit of anyone else. It may help the people you've harmed, but it will certainly make you feel like a new person! Besides, what we're doing in this step is getting ourselves to the point where we're ready and willing to apologize for our misdeeds. Whether or not making that apology is actually feasible is a question for later on.

Beginning with the Ones You Love

Do you remember the song, "You Always Hurt the One You Love"? That is true in more ways than one. Just about any police officer in the country can tell you that domestic violence is a real problem for the American people. Every year hundreds of women are battered and even killed by their husbands, and a smaller but significant number of men are murdered by their wives. Add to this the thousands of children who are victims of child abuse every year, and you can see what a problem it is.

You may be saying, "Wait a minute. This doesn't apply to me. I would never do anything to hurt my wife or my kids."

May be it's true that you would never lift a finger with the intention of inflicting physical harm, but there are other types of pain besides physical, and my own eyes and ears tell me that there are too many families today where love and respect have been replaced by sarcasm and cruelty.

A husband tears his wife apart with a malicious comment and then says, "I was only teasing. Can't you take a joke?"

A wife picks a public occasion to say something "witty" about her husband because it gets a big laugh, but it hurts his feelings, or she brings him down by complaining about his lack of material success.

Fathers pick on their kids, criticising instead of encouraging them.

That's the way it is in too many families today.

One of the reasons you always hurt the one you love is that you know how to do it. When you know someone that well, you know all of their "hot buttons" and vulnerabilities. It's easy, in the heat of an angry exchange, to go for the jugular. Far too many husbands and wives are ready to go for the jugular at the slightest provocation, and they often don't even realise what they've done.

When you hurt the one you love, you usually don't have to worry that the one you "pick on" is going to leave you because of the negative comments. If you treated a new friend or someone you'd just begun dating that way, they'd probably say something like, "Take a hike, I'm out of here," and end the relationship. A longtime, trusted friend or spouse will usually put up with quite a bit!

We have to change our hearts so that this kind of behaviour stops. If it's happened in the past, we've got to be willing to make it right. When you are preparing your list of those you have wronged, at the top of your list should be your spouse, your children, and other members of your immediate family. If after thinking and praying about it you feel that you've never done or said anything to hurt your spouse or your kids, muster up all the courage you have and ask them about it.

Also, ask your spouse if there's anything you do on a regular basis that causes her or him pain. Ask if there's anything you do that she really wishes you wouldn't do, and then turn it around and ask the reverse of that question — if there's anything you don't do that she really wants you to do.

I don't know why, but sometimes it's the hardest thing in the world to apologize to the people we love the best. That can be especially true of a parent, who believes that his children will lose respect for him if he apologizes to them. Nothing could be further from the truth. Apologizing to your children when you need to do so can really increase your standing in their eyes.

Here are some of the things for which you may need to apologize to your children:

- ❑ Being critical.
- ❑ Setting a bad example.
- ❑ Not spending enough time with them.
- ❑ Punishing them for something that wasn't really their fault, or punishing them too severely.
- ❑ Putting them down by your tone of voice or with words.

Think along those lines and examine your relationship with your children. Is it as it ought to be?

Is Restitution Necessary?

As you're preparing your list of people you have harmed, you may think of some situations where the damage you inflicted was more than emotional or mental. Did you cheat someone out of something he deserved? Did your personal habits result in a financial hardship for someone else? Did you steal? Did you destroy someone's property? If the answer to any of those questions is yes, then you may need to plan to make restitution — or at least offer to do so.

You may remember the story of Zacchaeus, the short man who climbed up in a sycamore tree because he wanted to get a glimpse of Jesus. He was so stunned he nearly fell out of that tree when Jesus looked up at him and said, "Zacchaeus, I'm coming to your house for dinner today." As stunned as Zacchaeus was, he wasn't any more surprised than some of the other people who witnessed the scene. They were wondering, "Doesn't Jesus know what sort of man he's talking to?" And no wonder because Zacchaeus was a tax collector, which was bad enough, and a dishonest one to boot! Yet Jesus knew exactly what He was doing and whom He was dealing with (He always does), and He was about to change this man's life forever.

After his dinner with Jesus, Zacchaeus had this to say:

> Look, Lord! Here and now I give half of my possessions to the poor, and if I have cheated anybody out of anything, I will pay back four times the amount.

And then Jesus, seeing that Zacchaeus' actions bore witness to his obvious change in attitude, responded, "Today salvation has come to this house."

It has been said that actions speak louder than words. It may be very difficult for you to tell someone you're sorry about something, but unless you demonstrate that you're willing to couple your words with action, the other person may doubt your sincerity. If, after examining the situation carefully, you honestly feel that you should offer to make restitution, then by all means do so.

Thinking about what you've done and who deserves your apology can be a painful process, but we're so far along the road now that it's much too late to turn back!

Victory is just ahead!

9

Time to Make Amends

Hundreds of people were there, crowded into the building and spilling out into the street, hoping to get a glimpse of the frail, white-haired gentleman, not wanting to miss a bit of the wisdom that would be in his words.

The place was Jerusalem. The time was nearly seventy years after the crucifixion and resurrection of Jesus Christ. The man this vast crowd had come to see was the apostle John, who was now nearly ninety years old.

He was stooped with age, and those who were closest to him could see that his hands shook, another indication of his advanced years.

The crowd was strangely silent as the people awaited John's sermon and listened to the introductory remarks about him. For most of the people gathered, there was a tremendous sense of awe as they thought about all the things John had seen with his own eyes. He was there when Jesus walked on water, when he raised Jairus' daughter from the dead, and when he took authority over the winds and waves.

John was present on the mountain when Jesus was transfigured. He was standing at the foot of the cross when the Lord was crucified. And then, three days later, he was the first to enter the empty tomb and see the evidence that Jesus had been raised from the dead. And, of course, he had been there when Christ ascended into the sky, promising that He would return someday in the very same way.

Finally, the introductory speaker finished his remarks and it was time for the great apostle to speak. With obvious effort, he rose to his feet and made his way to the front of the platform. He stood silently for a moment, and then said simply, "My children, love one another."

That was all. Having uttered those words, he turned and made his way back to his chair.

Church historians tell us that those five words made up the final public utterance of the apostle John. Undoubtedly, John knew that he was nearing the end of his life on earth, and he wanted to leave his listeners with something that was of vital importance.

He could have chosen to speak about the importance of holding to correct doctrine or living a pure life, and he undoubtedly could have gone on for hours, recounting many of the things he had seen and heard during the three years he spent with Christ.

But instead, he simply said, "Love one another."

The people of the first century desperately needed to hear and heed those words. The same is true for us who live in the first decade of the twenty first century. After all, human nature has changed very little over the last two thousand years.

Loving one another is really what the ninth step is all about.

Wherever it is possible, I will make direct amends to the people my behaviour has harmed.

It's caring enough about the other person to humbly attempt to make things right with him. It involves loving enough to risk being rejected. It is going to the person(s) you have wronged and saying, "I'm sorry for what I did. Will you please forgive me?"

When it's the hardest thing in the world to apologize or when you are tempted to hold on to resentment, remember those words from the apostle John, and seek to live up to them: "My children, love one another."

I've been asked before why this business of "making things right" should be so far along on the Twelve-Step journey to spiritual health. It's been suggested to me that it's so important it should be done sooner. The reason it has to wait until now is that our spiritual selves need time to mature. We have to wait until we have gained strength and confidence in our ability to eliminate negative characteristics in our lives. We have to wait until we can back up our apologies with evidence of changed lives. In other words, we have to be able to say, "I'm really sorry, and I don't know if I can stop, but I'm working on it," and be able to show by our actions that we mean it.

Before moving on, let's look back over where we've been so far. This is important. Each of the Twelve Steps builds on the previous step. This recap of what we've already discussed provides an opportunity for you to ask yourself if you've really done what each of these steps requires. If you haven't, go back and do it now. You can't skip a couple of steps and still expect to get maximum benefit from the process. You can't go back and take care of them later. If you want to reach your intended destination, you must follow the steps in the logical order in which they are presented. By reviewing the steps here you'll see the progress you've made.

First of all, we admitted that we were powerless by ourselves to get our lives to where they ought to be. After that, we acknowledged God's greatness and His ability to make us what we ought to be, and then we made the decision to turn our lives over to Him. For some of us, this was a first-time commitment, and for others of us it was a reaffirmation of an earlier decision, a re-acknowledgment that God loves us, wants only the best for us, and will bring good things into our lives if we will only let Him be the one in charge.

Having done that, we were free to make a close examination of our lives to see where we needed to change our behaviours. In step five, we admitted to God, ourselves, and to other people the exact nature of any defects in our character. After having taken that difficult step, we made ourselves entirely ready to have God remove those defects from our lives. In step seven we actually asked God to remove those shortcomings. Finally, in step eight, we turned our attention to others, making a list of the people we have harmed by our past behaviour and becoming willing to make amends to them.

Now, we are ready to carry out the things we became ready and willing to do in step eight.

It's Hard to Say "I'm Sorry"

You may remember Elton John's hit record of several years ago, "Sorry Seems to Be the Hardest Word." If you don't think human beings are born with a lot of pride in them, just ask a child to apologize to someone for something he did and watch how he reacts. Chances are very good that he'll cross his arms and become stiff. He'll pout and try to get out of the inevitable.

It's hard to get a child to admit that anything is his fault. I know that from practical experience. I don't care what is that my son, Anthony, has done. Somehow he'll find a way to blame it on his sister, Christina. You know the old story about George Washington and the cherry tree. When his father asked young George who had chopped down the tree, the boy replied, "I cannot tell a lie. I did it." Well, if Anthony had been George Washington he would have said something along the lines of "I cannot tell a lie. My sister, Christina, made me do it." Sometimes when I ask him why he did something he has a hard time figuring out a way to make his sister responsible, but he tries.

There's nothing unusual about that. It's very rare to find a child who doesn't want to find a way to put the blame on others. I always tell Anthony that when he's pointing the finger at his sister there are three fingers pointing right back at him. That's true for you and me, too. Besides, we are not children, and it's time for all of us to take a page out of George Washington's book, take the blame for our own actions, and be willing to apologize to those we have harmed, even though the child within wants to protect us by pointing the finger at others.

We tend to think that people will think less of us if we admit our mistakes. They'll like us less if we are able to say a heartfelt "I'm sorry." And that is simply not true. We all need to learn to be quick to say those two little words when we've done something wrong. Those of us who are parents need to say them to our children from time to time. (Yes, even parents make mistakes.) Husbands need to say them to their wives, wives to their husbands, bosses to their employees, employees to their bosses, and so on. What I'm saying here is that there isn't anybody in this world who's so big or so important or so anything else that he's above apologizing when he's made a mistake.

In the movie *Love Story* there's a line that says, "Love means never having to say you're sorry." Wrong! Love means you'll be the very first to admit it when you've done something wrong and to apologize to the one you love.

Do you remember the day President Nixon resigned? I remember what a sad day it was for this country that a president should be forced out of office. Now , I'm not sure what you think or thought of Richard Nixon. You may think he was a brilliant President or you may have a much lower opinion of him, but I honestly believe that if Mr. Nixon had taken some responsibility for the Watergate break-in and if he had said to Congress and the American people, "I'm very sorry about what happened," he might have been able to finish his term as President.

Instead, he refused to admit even the slightest bit of responsibility, and his presidency dissolved in a frenzy of finger-pointing, buck-passing, lying, and cover-up.

Understand that I'm not accusing Richard Nixon of anything. He did what he felt he had to do, but I believe that more openness and a willingness to apologise would have served him very well. There's a lesson in that for all of us.

Something We Should Have Learned in Kindergarten

A couple of years ago, there was a very popular book titled *All I Really Needed to Know I Learned in Kindergarten* by Robert Fulghum[1]. It was an enjoyable little book, with some good points about the importance of sharing and getting along with others.

As I write this my daughter Christina is in kindergarten, and her class has a rule that I think would be beneficial to the rest of us. That rule is that it is forbidden to say "I can't." Why? Because the person who says "I can't" is refusing to take responsibility for anything.

Some of us say "I can't" all the time. If not by our words, then certainly by our actions.

We say things like:

"I can't help the way I am."

"I can't change thing."

"I can't do any better."

"I can't try any harder."

"I can't stop myself from feeling this way."

I could probably go on for another ten pages or so, listing all the things we "can't" do. It's way past time to stop hiding behind those two little words. You can rise above making excuses for your actions, and do what you know ought to do.

When you were a child, I'm sure your parents read you the story about the little engine who thought he could. Perhaps you've even read it to your own kids. Remember how it goes? The little engine puffed up the hill and told himself over and over, "I think I can! I think I can!" And, sure enough, he does! That story became the basis for Andrew Lloyd Webber's hit musical *Starlight Express*, and one of the reasons that story has been around for so long is that it touches a chord of recognition in all of us.

What One Man Can Do

Not long ago I had the privilege of meeting a man who served this country during the Vietnam War. His name is John Keaveney, and even though he was born in Scotland, he believed in America so strongly and wanted to be an American so badly that he came to this country, enlisted in the Army, and wound up serving two tours in Vietnam. Like many Vietnam vets, Keaveney came home with severe emotional problems. He drank, he took drugs, he was unable to hold a job, and finally he wound up on the street. That's the way it was for more than eleven years — during which time he was in and out of jail, and his life was, by his own admission, one prolonged downward spiral.

This man was literally living in the gutter until a judge gave him a choice: a long jail term or enrolment in a Twelve-Step program. He chose the latter and with God's help was able to completely turn his life around. Now, this gentleman has put together a non-profit corporation to help the homeless.

He shared with me that there are 600,000 homeless Vietnam veterans living on the streets of this country today. Many of them are alcoholics. This is a tragic situation, and it's easy to see why and how it happened. Many of these men came home from Vietnam to a country that was either embarrassed by what they had done or else openly hostile to it. They had fought in a war where they never knew for sure who their enemy was and how or where he was going to strike. They fought in a brutal war where many of them saw their best friends killed, and many suffered painful and disabling injuries. Then they came home, and it seemed as though it was all for naught. Don't you think those are pretty good reasons to seek solace in a bottle or to be psychologically unable to hold onto a job? When you hold onto a reason long enough, however, it becomes an excuse.

I think it's terrible that this country hasn't done more for those who served in Vietnam, but at the same time, I admire this one Vietnam veteran who overcame being emotionally paralysed by the past and stopped saying, "I can't" and started saying, "I can." Because of that, he's making a difference in the world, and a great many homeless people are getting the help they need. He has started a program of housing, job training, and alcohol rehabilitation in the Los Angeles area and has put together a national coalition that provides services for homeless veterans in a number of other cities. With God's help, he has put his own life back together, and now he's making a difference for hundreds, and perhaps thousands, of others.

This ninth step is of vital importance because it's the point where we stop living in reaction to whatever has happened to us in the past and get on with living in the present and planning for the future.

If you think you can't, you won't; but if you think you can, well, you might surprise everyone. You can say, "I'm sorry for what I've done in the past, but it's going to be different from now on. I can and I will take responsibility for my actions."

Whatever needs to be done, whether it's making a phone call, writing a letter, paying a personal visit, or making restitution in some other way, make sure that everything is undergirded with prayer. Ask God to help you say and do the right things. Ask Him to prepare the hearts of the ones to whom you must apologize. And, finally, ask Him to give you the strength to take this painful step.

Keep in mind that your apology may not be accepted. If you call someone to say you're sorry, he might hang up on you before you get a chance to express yourself. You may never get a response to a letter you write. Someone may refuse to meet with you. If that's the case, it's certainly unfortunate, but you must be prepared for that sort of thing to happen. You can't let the other person's behaviour change your behaviour. At that point, it will be important for you to forgive the one who refuses to forgive you.

This is an excellent time to try to put into practice these words of Christ:

> Love your enemies, do good to those who hate you, bless those who curse you, pray for those who mistreat you. If someone strikes you on one cheek, turn to him the other also. If someone takes your cloak, do not stop him from taking your tunic. Give to everyone who asks you, and if anyone takes what belongs to you, do not demand it back. Do to others as you would have them do to you.

I know it's difficult to live up to those words. I won't pretend that I am able to live up to them seven days a week, twenty-four hours a day, but that's the goal we all should have — especially those last eleven words: "Do to others as you would have them do to you."

The Importance of the Horizontal

Several times during the course of this book, I've mentioned my friend John C. When he reached this point in his Twelve-Step program he had quite a bit of fence-mending to do. Two areas were very serious.

The first had to do with the law. He had been charged with drunk driving — for the fifth time — and hadn't shown up for his hearing. He had to go now and confess, even though he knew he would wind up in jail.

"I went to my probation officer and told him I was sorry that I hadn't shown up but that I was into

AA and trying to get my life together." To John's surprise, the officer just chuckled and said, "Well, just come pay the rest of your fine when you can."

John was amazed and delighted by that reaction, but then he had to turn his attention to another matter.

During World War II he had become involved in a relationship with a woman who was engaged to another man. They had carried on a torrid affair until the young woman's fiance returned from overseas duty, and the couple was married.

During one of their first fights after their wedding, the woman told her husband all about her affair with John. Upon hearing this, her husband stormed over to John's house, and threatened his life.

"He told me to stay out of his sight or he was going to kill me," John says. "He was a big, strong, hot-tempered guy, and I believed him, so from then on I went out of my way to avoid him.

"Only now, I had to go talk to him and let him know that I was sorry for what I had done — and that I simply wasn't going to avoid him any longer. It wasn't easy — believe me."

Again, John got an amazing response.

"Oh... geeze..." the big guy said. "I didn't mean any of what I said. Don't worry about it. Sure, I forgive you."

John says, "I couldn't believe it. I'd been drinking to hide from so many of these things, and I should have just dealt with them to begin with."

Through the process of making reconciliation, John says he developed a brand new faith in human beings. "I found out that people aren't so bad!"

He also found his relationship with God improving.

It always amazes me when people seem to think their relationship with God has nothing at all to do with anyone else. It's terribly inconsistent to be sitting in a church singing praises to God while we harbour anger and resentment toward an ex-spouse, a neighbour, or an associate.

One way of looking at this is to say that our vertical relationship (with God up there and us down here) can't be right unless our horizontal relationships (with our fellow human beings) are right, too.

> Jesus said:
>
> If you are offering your gift at the altar and there remember that your brother has something against you, leave your gift there in front of the altar. First go and be reconciled to your brother; then come and offer your gift.

Now it may be that your brother won't listen to you. You may tell him you're sorry, only to have him respond with an emphatic, "Drop dead!" That is something over which you have no control. The important thing is that you have done what's right you have done your best to get that horizontal relationship in order. Getting your horizontal relationships in order may mean asking for forgiveness, or it may mean extending forgiveness to others.

Jesus also said:

> Love your enemies, do good to those who hate you, bless those who curse you, pray for those who mistreat you.

The Lord's Prayer is an illustration of the importance of the horizontal relationship, for it ties together God's forgiveness of our sins with our own willingness to forgive the sins of others against us — asking God to forgive our debts in the same way that we forgive our debtors.

Believe me, I know how hard it is to bless those who curse you and pray for those who mistreat you. Nevertheless, that is the attitude God expects of us. As John C. says, "You've got to forgive. It's hard work carrying around a bunch of resentments, and it's bound to destroy you."

I would go so far as to say that there's not a person alive today — including me — who doesn't need to make amends with someone. The beautiful thing about step nine is that it helps us deal with those past failures that have haunted us and enables us to move on into a healthy and rewarding future. It gives us the ability to begin to rebuild our self-esteem and to achieve a peaceful relationship with ourselves, our fellow human beings, and our God.

It would be impossible for me to overstate the importance of this step. Here is an opportunity for us to clear the garden of our lives of weeds and dead leaves, to rake up and discard all of the old hurts and difficulties once and for all.

If you've ever spent a day getting a garden ready — hoeing, raking and pulling weeds — you know what hard work it can be. After several hours of that sort of labour, dozens of muscles you didn't even know you had will hurt. As you look over what you've accomplished, however, you'll have a sense of self-satisfaction that makes all those aching muscles worthwhile. In the same way, it is not easy to make amends for wrongs you've committed, but that, too, is more than worth the effort. That's something I recently found out for myself when a situation developed that left me hurt and angry toward a longtime friend.

My friend's father, F.E., though quite a few years older than I, was also a very good friend of mine. Actually, he was more than a friend. He was always there for me — to congratulate me when I was doing well and to offer a few words of encouragement when I was struggling. We talked on the phone frequently, and we wrote to each other on a regular basis.

Every time I spoke on the *Hour of Power broadcast*, I could count on getting a telephone call from him the following morning, and he'd always start off by saying something like, "I sure enjoyed your message yesterday." You know the type of person he was. There could never be enough people like him, and I always considered it a blessing to know him.

He was in his eighties when he contracted pneumonia and died. His passing hit me pretty hard. His family decided not to have a funeral or memorial service for him. They had something very small and private, with only the immediate family members in attendance. This made my sense of loss even greater. There is something about a funeral that gives closure to a relationship and aids the grief process. It's a chance to pay respect and to say, "so long until we meet again." I felt cheated out of a chance to tell my old friend good-bye.

Because of my hurt and anger, I didn't tell my friend that I sympathised with him over the loss of his father. I saw him occasionally and always smiled and said something like, "It's really good to see you," but I never once said a word to him concerning how bad I felt about his dad's death.

I'm sure he must have thought it was a bit cold or unfeeling not to even mention it. He probably wondered how I could be so nonchalant about his dad's death when we had been good friends. My hurt feelings were more powerful than my desire to do the right thing and extend my sympathy.

The situation bothered me enough to wake me up at night, so I decided that I really needed to take steps to make things right. It was during one of those sleepless nights that I got out of bed and wrote my friend a letter, explaining everything to him. I told him that I was angry with him and that I was sorry for my anger. I apologized for never consoling him and being a pastor to him. I promised him that my actions would be different toward him from then on. The next time I saw him, I would tell him personally what a great sense of loss I felt when his father died, and I'd ask him how he was coping with his loss. I also said that I knew we would have a different relationship — a better relationship — than we'd ever had before.

It wasn't easy to write that letter. Even though I had known it was the right thing to do, it still took me some time to become willing to do it. Once I became willing, I almost couldn't do it fast enough. In fact, I woke at 2:00 A.M. and knew I had to do it or I wouldn't get any more sleep the rest of the night. As I wrote that letter, through my tears, I was healed of the angry, resentful feelings I had carried around for several weeks. I later discovered that my actions hadn't hurt my friend nearly as much as they had hurt me. In reaching out to make peace with him, I found peace for myself.

That almost always happens when you forget about yourself and reach out to someone else — and especially someone you may have hurt in the past. You receive healing and peace, and the unresolved guilt that has held you back and caused difficulties in your life is removed. This, in turn, leads to increased self-esteem, and you are better able to interact positively with others.

I heard a story that illustrates perfectly this idea of being blessed by coming to the place of putting others' needs ahead of our own. I'm not sure where I heard the story, and I don't know when or where it happened — so I can't vouch for its authenticity — but it's supposed to be a true story, an I tend to believe it.

It seems a man became very ill and was rushed to the hospital. He had a temperature of nearly 107 degrees, and though his doctors and nurses tried everything they could think of to break that fever, it just wouldn't come down. They knew he would not be able to survive for long in that condition, and even if he did, severe brain damage was likely to result. As you can imagine, during this time of crisis, the sick man's thoughts were centered entirely on himself. Over and over he pleaded, "God help me!" but nothing seemed to happen.

And then, during the middle of a fitful night, he happened to look across the room and see that he now had a roommate. Even though he felt absolutely terrible, he realised that he couldn't possibly feel as awful as this new fellow did. This man was very pale and had hollow, sunken eyes. He was obviously suffering a great deal. You've heard the expression, "death warmed over." That's what this man looked like, and it didn't seem very likely that he was going to survive the night.

For a brief instant, the first man forgot about his own problems and asked God to bless the other man. "Lord," he said, "I can't stand to see this fellow suffer like this. I've been asking you over and over to heal me. But now I tell you that I don't care what happens to me, but please help him."

After praying that prayer, he drifted off to sleep and, for the first time in a while, slept soundly for several hours. When he finally awoke, sunlight was streaming through the window, and he immediately noticed two things. One, he felt much better.

Two, the other man was gone.

When the doctor came in on his rounds, he was surprised and delighted to see his patient doing so well. The fever had broken during the night, and the prognosis was excellent for a complete and speedy recovery.

"That's great," the man said, "but what about the other man who was in here last night? Did he... die?"

The doctor looked perplexed. "What man?" he asked. "Who else was in here last night?"

"The other patient."

"There's never been any patient in this room but you."

"But he was right over there." The man gestured in the direction of the person he had seen, but there was nothing there now, nothing but a window.

It took them a while to figure out exactly what had happened, but they finally came to this conclusion. All during the night, the curtains on the window had remained open. Somehow, the conditions were just right so that when the sick man looked at the window, he saw his own reflection, and in his feverish state, he thought he was looking at another man. As he unselfishly forgot about himself and reached out to someone else, he actually brought God's blessing into his own life. He got his life back when he was willing to let go of it to help someone else.

I think that's almost always what happens when we forget about our own hurts and our own needs and focus instead on healing the hurts and meeting the needs of others. That's why it's so important to go back and make amends to those we've wronged in some way. Not only does it bless the one with whom we've had a problem, but it brings healing to us, as well.

The first thing you must do in order to make amends to someone you've wronged is to take responsibility for your own actions. You can't say, "It's not my fault," or "He deserved it."

Have you ever tried to break up a fight between a couple of small children? Ask them who started it, and the response goes something like this:

"He did!"

"I did not! She did!"

"Did not!"

"Did so!"

"Did not!"

And on and on they will go, each one refusing to acknowledge the part he or she played in starting a mini-war.

Whether or not the other person is guilty of wrongdoing, we must concentrate on our own shortcomings and not his. In other words, we must take responsibility for our own actions, and we must make restitution for those actions.

The Ghosts of Unresolved Guilt

In his play *Julius Caesar,* William Shakespeare wrote these lines:

The evil that men do lives after them,
The good is oft interred with their bones.

Certainly that's a pessimistic view of things, and it's an idea that's not in keeping with the Christian view of a God who is a redeemer and who is always ready to forgive.

Yet, wouldn't it be terribly sad to be nearing the end of your life and realise that there were people to whom you needed to apologise and make restitution? Wouldn't it be sad to think, at that stage of your life, about people you had hurt and wrong things you'd done that you had never even attempted to correct?

That would be especially painful if you realised that any chance to make restitution had passed you by — that it was too late. Would you be worried that some of the evil things you had done would live on, after you were gone?

That's just another reason why it's so important to do your best, right now, to make things right so that you can live in peace the rest of your life — so that, when the time comes, you can leave this world with a clean heart and a clear conscience.

That was brought home to me in movie called *Flatliners* that I happened to see a couple of years ago. The story was about a group of medical students who were conducting experiments to experience temporary death, so they could then explain what it's like. Driven by curiosity and spurred on by numerous accounts of near-death experiences, they had devised a way to actually take a person to the point of physical death for a few minutes, and then, at precisely the right moment, bring him back. (In medical terminology, "flatlining" occurs at the point of death. It's when there is no heartbeat, no respiration, no brainwaves — nothing but a flat line registered by all of those machines and gauges hooked up to the body.)

One by one, the students volunteered to "die" for a few minutes, just to see what lies beyond this life. In each case the student was met on "the other side" by some situation revolving around unresolved guilt. You might say that they were attacked by the ghosts of the past. Each one came face to face with someone he had hurt in some way, someone to whom an apology had never been given nor restitution offered. Then each ghost from the past followed the "flatliner" back into the physical world, where he continued to haunt him and remind him of the harmful things he had done.

At first, some of the students pretended not to understand why they were being harassed; but in reality they knew why it was happening and what they had to do about it.

Eventually, one by one, the medical students began to make amends for the things they had done. And, as a result, by movie's end they were all happier, healthier, more peaceful people.

The movie reminds us that whether we want to admit it or not, if there is unresolved guilt and conflict in our lives, it will not let go. It will continue to haunt us until we take steps toward making things right.

As you move along the path to making thing right, here are some things to keep in mind:

- ❑ You must be willing to forgive yourself and the other person.
- ❑ Pray the situation through *before* you approach the offended party. Know what you want to say and how you want to react to any response he might make.
- ❑ Your attempt to make amends must focus on your behaviour and not on the behaviour of the other person.
- ❑ Your apology should be as simple and straight forward as possible. You do not have to go into every minute detail of the situation that developed between the two of you.
- ❑ If the other person doesn't seem to know how to respond, don't push for a specific answer.

Your actions is what's important, not the response from the other person.

- ❑ If you find that you are unable to approach someone to whom amends are due, go back to step four.

A Time to Keep Things to Yourself

There are times when taking steps toward making things right may not include an apology. This is especially true in a situation where you know what you've done to hurt another person, but he or she doesn't know — and would only be hurt by finding out about it.

Certainly, someone who has hurt his mate in this way needs to confess his sin to God and to another human being — preferably a pastor or professional counsellor who will not be tempted to turn it into neighbourhood gossip. He also needs to try to understand the motivation for his behaviour. If you see that you have done things to hurt your mate in the past, resolve to build a better future between you by seeking the counsel of a good therapist and by working through the Twelve Steps to overcome the unresolved issues of your life together.

Not too long ago there was a movie called *Scenes from a Mall* about a man who decided, in the middle of a large shopping mall, to confess to his wife that he had been involved in an affair. He knew she would be able to accept it and forgive him. After all, she was a nationally famous psychologist whose advice had saved numerous marriages. But, of course, she couldn't handle the news as well as he thought she could, and forgiving him was anything but easy. The movie wasn't all that great, but it did make the point that open confession of past transgressions isn't always the best path to take. And, even though this movie was a comedy, a real life situation of this sort is certainly more of a tragedy.

You can probably think of some other times when it would not be a good idea to go directly to the party you have wronged with your confession. Almost always, the decision to confess should be based on whether it will do good or harm.

It might also be necessary to refrain from an open confession of the wrong you have committed against someone, if that confession would harm an innocent third party in some way. You should examine the situation carefully to make sure you're holding back because you're worried about the other person's welfare — and not your own.

There may also be situations when you know that you would be hurting the other person merely by trying to talk to him about the wrong you committed. If that's the case, you need to do three things:

1. Be patient as you await the proper time to approach the person with your apology.
2. Pray for a softening of the other person's heart.
3. Look for opportunities to reopen lines of communication.

In obeying God's Word, we are to make amends but we are also to deal with each other in love.

> Let no debt remain outstanding, except the continuing debt to love one another, for he who loves his fellowman has fulfilled the law.

An Apology Isn't Enough

Before we move on to the tenth of our Twelve Steps, I think it's important to remind you that there is a difference between making an apology and making amends or restitution for your actions. An apology is merely saying, "I'm sorry." Making amends goes further than that. It makes sure our harmful actions are never repeated.

Suppose you caught me lying to you about something, but I told you that I was sorry and asked you to forgive me, so you did. The very next day you caught me in another lie. Again, I offered my apology, and expressed my regret about the way I had been acting. And then, once again, turned right around and told you a whopper for the third consecutive day. By that time you would undoubtedly and understandably be very reluctant to accept my apology because I had shown you that it wasn't sincere. I had made no attempt to make amends to you. When you're truly sorry about something, you will do your best to avoid repeating it.

If I were an employee who came to work late every day, my boss would very quickly tire of hearing my apologies and would tell me that unless I changed my ways, I was going to be standing in the unemployment line. He'd expect me to make amends for my past tardiness by being promptly on time from then on.

There are two old proverbs that do a pretty good job of describing what I'm talking about. The first is: "Talk is cheap." The second is: "Actions speak louder than words."

It's also been said that "if you're going to talk the talk, you need to walk the walk," and I think that sums it up very well. Don't just say you want to make things right. Show by your actions that it's so. Remember, our walk talks, and our talk walks — but our walk talks further than our talk walks!

The Danger of Losing Ground

Sometimes, people are held back from making amends by the fear that they'll be hurting themselves. The truth is just the opposite. If you don't make amends when you need to, you are not going to feel the peace and serenity God has for you. You will begin regressing spiritually, emotionally, and physically.

Fear causes us to say things like "let sleeping dogs lie," or "let bygones be bygones." Yet those are impossible things to do if the worms of guilt and sorrow are eating away at the heart, soul, and spirit. The only way to overcome those destructive worms is to move ahead with the task of making amends where you need to make them.

Looking back over these first nine of the Twelve Steps, I'm sure you can see why they are so effective when it comes to changing lives. They work because they are tough. This is no easy path we're on, but it's an effective one, and if you follow it carefully, your destination is certain: a life of peace, joy, and freedom.

In spite of your progress through the Twelve-Step program, your tendency will be to fall back on old habits and ways of dealing with threatening situations. You can succeed, but it will require work, and you might fail from time to time. Don't judge yourself too harshly, but don't shrug things off, either.

When you fail, examine yourself to see why. Ask God to forgive you and give you the strength to do better in the future. You'll also need to look closely at your life to see if the inventory you prepared in step four was really as complete as you thought it was. You may need to take another look at step six to see if there is some defect in your character that you have not yet relinquished to God's control.

Before you move on to the next step, I want you to follow through on what we've talked about in this chapter:

- ❑ Write the letter you need to write.
- ❑ Make that phone call that you've been putting off for so long.
- ❑ Make a commitment to reach out to all of those to whom you need to make amends.

Now, as you prepare to take steps to bridge the gap that exists between you and those who have been hurt by your past actions.

I invite you to pray the following prayer with me.

> *Dear Heavenly Father, I pray that you will continue to help me discard all of the bad habits and bad feelings that I have been holding on to. Help me to take the responsibility for restoring those whom I have offended. Lead me and guide me so that I may achieve proper relationships with others. I love you and I praise your name.* Amen.

10

Keeping Your House in Order

Do you ever forget to take out the trash? I do. In my neighbourhood, the city garbage trucks come around one day every week — and your garbage had better be out on the curb waiting. If it isn't, there's nothing you can do but wait until the following week, when garbage day rolls around once again.

Not too long ago, I forgot to put the garbage out on the curb for three weeks in a row. It was just one of those times when there were so many other things going on in my life that "garbage day" just didn't register. As you can imagine, by garbage day of the fourth week, we had quite a collection of trash sitting in our garage. And to put it as mildly as possible, it wasn't smelling very good. There was no way I could forget to put it out this time.

Then I looked at the calendar and noticed that garbage day happened to fall on Memorial Day that week. Whenever garbage day fell on a national holiday, garbage pickup was usually delayed for a day

— although you couldn't always be sure. I certainly didn't want to chance anything, because another week with all of that garbage in the garage would really be unbearable.

My usual routine is to take the garbage out to the street the night before the garbage truck comes, and most of my neighbours do the same thing. That's because the truck comes very early in the morning. So the night before what would have been pick-up day, I went outside and looked up and down the street. Garbage cans sat in front of five or six homes on my nineteen-home culde-sac. The evidence was inconclusive, but based on what the majority of my neighbours had done, I assumed that trash collection would be postponed a day.

I went on in the house and went to bed, prepared for a good night's sleep. Sometime around 3 A.M. I was awakened by a strange sound. I thought I heard the whirring and banging of the city garbage truck — off in the distance — as it was making its way toward my neighbourhood! Not only was the truck coming, but it was coming much earlier than usual!

I sat up in bed and listened. There was nothing. It must have been my imagination. I settled back into bed, but all of a sudden there it was again — that banging and changing, and it was getting closer.

I got out of bed, set the world record for speed-dressing, and went outside. Then I couldn't be sure. Did I hear the garbage truck, or didn't I?

I didn't know what to do, so I actually got in my car and drove around the neighbourhood, looking for the garbage truck. And this was at 3 A.M.! I thought

I heard it down this street, and then that one, but it was nowhere in sight.

I went home, put my head back on my pillow, and heard the noise again. Every time I lay down I was haunted by the garbage ghost. Finally I was able to convince myself that it was my imagination and drifted off to sleep. I did not forget to put the garbage out on the curb for the truck to pick up the following day!

There was a great lesson here for me: We must dispose of our garbage on a regular basis — whether we're talking about physical garbage or garbage of any other variety. If you don't take out the garbage regularly, it's going to rot, it's going to stink, and you won't be able to sleep at night.

This is what step ten is all about.

I will continue to take personal inventory
of my life on a regular basis and
promptly admit it when I do something
wrong or lapse back into old behaviour
pattern.

Regular Maintenance

Time for a quickie quiz. See if you can finish the old rhyme:

A man may work from sun to sun
But a woman's work ________.

Did you get it? The correct answer is "is never done." The truth in this rhyme is that a typically man's workday starts when he goes to the job in the morning and is over when he comes home at night. A typical woman is always at it, from the moment she gets out of bed in the morning until the moment she falls exhausted back into the same bed at night. In other words, house-work never takes a vacation. There's always something to be done — dusting, vacuuming, mopping, straightening, and on and on.

Today the rhyme may be pretty much outdated. These days a lot of men are realizing that they have to pitch in and help with the housework, too. It is not women's work but something the husband and wife should share, especially if she, too, is working outside the home.

Whoever does it, cleaning must be done on a regular basis. If you don't mop the floor, it will soon be so dirty that you can't get it clean with just a mop. If you don't vacuum the carpet regularly, you can imagine how messy it would soon look. What about the front lawn? What would it look like if you decided that you'd let it grow for a couple of months in the summer? More than likely you'd wind up losing your lawnmower in the tall grass.

There's a house near where I live that's been on the market for quite awhile. The last time I drove by there, the front yard looked terrible. It was all grown up with weeds, and it's going to take quite a bit of work to get it into decent shape. That's what happens when things are not cared for. They fall apart, they are covered with dirt, or they are taken over by weeds.

Regarding that empty house, soon the owner is going to have to hire a gardener to come take care of that yard. I know what that gardener is going to think when he sees the shape the yard is in. His first thought will be, "Oh, no! Why didn't they call me sooner?"

Regular maintenance is much easier than letting things go and then trying to get caught up all at once. There is always a terrible price to pay for neglect or laziness. That's what last three of our Twelve Steps are all about — regular maintenance — making sure we are following the path we have set for ourselves.

At this point, someone may say, "If I'm set free from those old character defects, then why do I have to worry about regular maintenance? If I'm free, I'm free, right?"

Fallible human nature is very strong. Our tendency to sin is strong. Our ability to resist is weak. There will always be fears and cares and situations that can pull us back into our old lifestyle. Being vigilant is much better than being overconfident.

The Bible says that "pride goes before destruction" and that is often true.

Don't Stop Now!

What I've seen happen is that when people get all the way to step ten, they think they've got it made — that the journey toward wholeness is complete. But it isn't. It may even be the most dangerous time of the journey. The normal human tendency is to lapse back into old habits and ways of thinking without even realising what's happened.

The person who has successfully completed the first nine of the Twelve Steps feels good because his life is going along better than it ever has before. He's free from pain. He's comfortable, but there's something to be said for never letting yourself get too comfortable. I suggest that you take some time every day to make a spot check and see how you're doing. Think back over the things you're doing. Think back over the things you've done and said and the ways you've reacted to certain situations. Are you really living the way you want to live?

Try to find some quiet time near the end of the day where you can be alone — in the car driving home from work, during your shower or bath, before you fall asleep — and quietly review everything that's happened to you during the previous twenty-four hours. Ask yourself a few questions:

- Were there specific situations that I did not handle well? (This will show you some areas where you still need to grow).
- Were there specific situations that I handled particularly well? (Don't hesitate to give yourself a pat on the back if you deserve it!)
- Were there any situations today that tempted me to fall back into my old behaviour patterns? If so, what were those situations, and why did they affect me the way they did? These are situations that should be avoided.
- What can I learn from the experiences I had today?
- What should I do differently tomorrow?

Besides stopping at the end of each day, I also recommend periodic spot checks throughout the day. You've seen the bumper stickers that some trucking companies put on their vehicles: "How am I driving?" There's an 800 number to call if you have any comments on the way the truck is being driven. That's the way you need to view your life — as if you're wearing a "How am I doing?" bumper sticker. You have to occasionally stop and answer that question for yourself. How are you doing now that you decided to let God control your life? If you see something wrong, don't let it go. Do your best to take care of it immediately.

Ephesians 4 talks about being careful not to give the devil a foothold in your life by letting "the sun go down while you are still angry" about something. When I was a boy, my parents made me live up to that verse. Whenever I had a fight with my sister, I had to make up with her before I was allowed to go to bed. It didn't matter how tired I was — or how angry I was. The two of us had to get things right between us before the day was over, and that was all there was to it. I'm glad my parents felt so strongly about the danger of letting anger fester. I know for certain that the best way to deal with any problem area in your life is immediately, before it grows into something that's nearly unmanageable.

In addition to taking inventory at the end of each day, and occasional spot checks throughout the day, I also advise you to periodically spend some time going back over the inventory you prepared in step four. Have you made as much progress as you would like in those areas that once gave you so much trouble? I sincerely hope that when you review the progress you've made you're able to say, "I'm doing great." If you're not doing great, don't despair, and don't be too harsh on yourself. If you see that you're falling short, this is the time to rededicate yourself to the task at hand. You may need to carefully go back through some of the steps to get back on course. Recommit yourself to finishing this journey. You can do it!

Periodic Spot Checks

I've recently discovered that "spot check inventories" should include taking a look at your physical well-being. Perhaps I shouldn't say I've just discovered it because I've known it for some time, but only within the last few years have I been putting into practice what I knew.

The Bible says:

> Do you not know that your body is a temple of the Holy Spirit, who is in you, whom you have received from God?

If you seek to honour God with your body, you'll take care of it and keep it in the best possible shape. You won't take it for granted or do things to harm it.

This is all part of a healthy lifestyle. The person who takes care of his body will be healthier than the one who doesn't. That means he'll feel better and be happier and, as a result, be more apt to bring honour to God.

Up until about three years ago, I wasn't paying much attention to my body. I didn't eat right or exercise. Then I went in for a complete physical and got a little surprise when the doctor told me that my cholesterol level was above normal and that I'd need to watch it. Well, it wasn't really that high, so I didn't worry about it too much. Guess what happened the next time I went in. My cholesterol level was even higher — quite a bit higher, in fact.

That woke me up. I knew I was going in the wrong direction, so I started to read up on how I could lower my cholesterol, and that in turn led me into a study of the entire subject of nutrition. I came to the realisation that if you want to live a healthy life you have to "eat healthy." Eating means developing proper eating habits. For me, it means eating bread without butter on it and pizza without cheese on it and doing without some things I used to like but which plainly were having an adverse affect on my body. I didn't go on a diet, but I did change my eating habits. I lost ten pounds of fat without trying, and I feel much better today as a result.

Not too long ago, I went to my doctor for a physical, and he told me that 9 percent of my body weight consists of fat. The ideal body fat level for a man is 5 to 10 percent, whereas the average is 26 percent. People don't understand exercise and good nutrition. Often when people start to put on weight, they make the mistake of immediately going on a diet. The problem is that if you're on a diet your body chooses to burn muscle instead of fat. You'll lose some weight, all right, but if you take a body-fat test you'll find that your body-fat percentages have actually gone up. When you get tired of the diet and go back to your old way of eating, you'll find that you're likely to gain all that weight back very quickly, only this time you'll be gaining fat instead of muscle. It is actually possible for someone to be quite thin and still have way too much in the way of body fat. They are what health experts call "fat skinny people."

It may seem that I've gotten a little far afield here, but my point is that we need to take spot checks of every part of our lives — physical as well as behavioural. You can't expect to be physically healthy if you don't watch your diet and exercise. You can't expect to be spiritually healthy if you don't regularly pay attention to spiritual things: Did I remember to pray today, to communicate with my Creator? You can't expect to be emotionally healthy if you don't spot check your actions: Have I offended someone today? Have I done anything to hurt someone? Have I reverted to any of those old ways I want so much to be rid of?

Write It Down

Let me tell you about something else I started doing about a year or so ago. I started keeping a journal. On a daily basis, I take about fifteen minutes to write down all the things I've done with my day. This is my personal journal, only for my eyes, so I can and do write down my innermost thoughts. I record what I've eaten and what I've done: the mistakes I've made, the people I may have offended, and the things I feel good about.

The process of keeping a journal has been enjoyable, and by keeping a record of each day's events and my thoughts and feelings, I've learned a great deal about myself.

Recently, I spent a couple of days with my father. The first evening, I was writing in my journal when he came in and asked me what I was doing. When I explained that I started keeping a journal, he said, "You know, I wish I'd started that when I was your age. Just think how valuable that would be to me now."

I agreed with him. "You've got a point there, Dad. Now, how long did you say you were planning on living?"

"Oh... to ninety-five or one hundred."

"That's what I thought. And how old are you now?"

He wasn't biting. "I know what you're getting at, Robert. Now lay off!"

I said, "How valuable do you think a journal of the next thirty years of your life would be?"

Well, I'm not sure he took me up on it, but I hope he did because reading back through a journal can be a valuable experience. I don't know how old you are, but I guarantee you that you're not too old to start keeping a journal. In the short-term, this presents an opportunity for you to take a daily inventory. As the days go by, it can assist you in taking a long-term inventory. Look at your attitudes of last month or last week. What were the things you did that you wish you hadn't? Can you see that you're making sufficient progress? Do you see areas where you repeatedly fall short? The human memory can be a funny thing. Our brains can be very selective about what they choose to remember. If you've written things down honestly, however, the truth is there for you to review.

A Change Has Taken Place

There was a time in the life of Rancho Capistrano Community Church when I felt frustrated with the way things were going. There wasn't anything terribly wrong. It was just that we weren't making much progress. We had reached a plateau, and it seemed that we couldn't go any further. We weren't growing in numbers, I didn't see people's lives being changed for the better, and I was discouraged.

I made a decision at that time that I would attend a seminar or retreat every single month. I did that for at least a year and a half. Sometimes I had a one-day retreat, and other times I went to a three- or four-day seminar. When I did that, I began to grow in a way I never had before because I was taking periodic spot checks of my life and making whatever changes and adjustments were necessary. The results have been remarkable. Within two years, the church got off the plateau and nearly doubled in size. Prayer became a central focus, with groups meeting every night and lives being changed.

Step ten tells us to take an honest look at ourselves, and keep on taking honest looks at ourselves, so that we know precisely how we're doing on our spiritual journey. We need to be careful not to become too smug about our successes or too devastated by our failures. Both successes and failures are signposts to guide us on our way.

It would be virtually impossible for me to overemphasise the importance of periodically taking inventory of your life. As you do, you should find beneficial changes taking place.

- You should have fewer problems with relationships since you are more apt to admit it when you have been wrong.
- You don't have to worry about being "found out" and can face the future with fearless honesty.
- You no longer have to make any pretence of perfection, either in front of others or in front of yourself.
- As you better understand yourself and your own behaviour, you are also better able to understand the behaviour of others and deal with them on an open and accepting basis.

We have now taken ten steps. There are two more to go. Let's move on to step eleven.

11
Get Closer to God

Not too long ago, I happened to see this message on a sign in front of a little church: "If God seems farther away these days, guess who moved."

That's a pretty good thought. There are times for all of us when God seems to be on vacation, when the heavens seem to be like brass and our prayers don't go any farther than the ceiling.

The absolute truth is that God doesn't change. He's always there, always ready to listen, always ready to demonstrate His love to those who seek Him. The difference is that people change. Some days we're on top of the world and feel like we could lick ten times our weight in mountain lions. Other days we're so far down in the valley that we'd need a ten-foot pole just to reach up and touch the bottom. Some days we think we have enough faith to go into the lions' den with the prophet Daniel. Other days, we feel like Peter in the courtyard, cursing and swearing and denying Christ.

Admittedly, there is no one in the world who doesn't have his bad days. It's all part of life on this planet, and Jesus Himself promised us that we weren't going to go sailing through a life of ease, like Huck Finn and Tom Sawyer drifting leisurely down the Mississippi River. The rain falls on the just and the unjust alike.

Step eleven says:

I will seek to know more of God.

In other words, I will seek to improve my relationship with God, praying for knowledge of His will and the power to carry it out.

If, as you've read this book, you've been serious about putting these Twelve Steps into practice, you've already come a very long way on your journey toward spiritual wholeness. Looking over your current attitudes and behaviours and contrasting them with your attitudes and behaviours of the past, you're bound to feel good. And rightly so! It's great to see your life shaping into what you've always known it should be. We all need to keep in mind that we have never really arrived at perfection. Life brings us many opportunities to fall or succeed, and we must be on constant watch. That means we're constantly going to need God's help and that, in turn, means that we need to be as close to Him as we can possibly be.

Here is my favourite definition of the word success: "Success is not a destination. Rather, it is a journey; a way of life." That definition applies directly to what we're trying to do through these Twelve

Steps. We're not trying to reach some destination — perfection, or spiritual maturity, or whatever you want to call it. We're trying to change the way we make our journey through this life, making sure we do our best to live each day as God would have us.

Only When Things Go Wrong

On any trip into unfamiliar territory, it's easy to take a wrong turn and get lost for awhile. Let me tell you that this is especially true in Southern California, where we seem to have almost as many freeways as we do people. Sometimes, in order to get from one place to another only fifteen or twenty miles away, Southern Californians may have to travel on as many as four or five freeways. It can be terribly confusing — especially to newcomers. Not only that, but if you happen to blink at the wrong time, you might miss the exit you need and not be able to turn around and get going in the right direction until you're several miles farther on down the road. Taking a wrong road or missing your exit doesn't mean you've blown your entire trip, however, just that you're going to be inconvenienced for a few minutes. It is possible to redirect yourself and get going in the right direction again.

My point is that you shouldn't be furious with yourself and feel that you've ruined things if you goof once in a while and do something you know you shouldn't do, say something you shouldn't say, or think something you shouldn't think. I'll say it again: We all take wrong turns now and again, and the only thing to do when that happens is to turn around and get back on the right road.

I wouldn't want you to misunderstand me and think that your life is going to be perfect if you're spending as much time as you can getting close to God and working at the Twelve Steps. None of us will have perfect lives this side of heaven. I do believe that your life will be better if you seek to stay close to Him and that you'll have the serenity and joy of knowing that God is with you and that His hand is guiding you, even during the toughest of times.

Furthermore, I believe that God's presence in your life will result in greater health and wealth. These things will be the direct result of peace of mind and clarity of vision and purpose. It is only natural and realistic that the emotional wellness that comes from living close to God will produce greater benefits in all areas of life. But don't make the mistake of seeking blessings—such as financial well-being. Instead, seek God's will for your life, and He will bless you in the ways that are best for you.

If you are living close to God, I know without any hesitation, that He is blessing you. He is blessing you by giving you the knowledge that you're living the life He planned for you, by making you aware of His presence in your life, and by filling your heart and soul with "the peace of God, which transcends all understanding".

You may not be as wealthy, healthy or happy as you want or think you should be, but surely you are wealthier, healthier, and happier than you would be if you hadn't worked through the steps and moved closer to God. There cannot be anything better than being aware of God's presence with you on a daily

basis. Anything else pales by comparison, almost to the point of disappearing.

How do you get closer to God? I believe there are at least four specific ways, all of which are interrelated and may overlap in places. They are:

Prayer
Meditation
Reading the Scriptures
Spending time with other believers

All of these activities should be undertaken on a regular basis. Let's examine each of them in greater detail.

Prayer

The Bible tells us that we should "pray continually", or, as the King James Version has it, "pray without ceasing." That's very good advice. We need to remember to pray all the time, about every struggle we're facing, every decision we have to make. God cares. Don't ever think that you're bothering Him about something, no matter how trivial you may think your problem seems when compared with everything else that's going on in the world. God wants you to talk to Him about it. He always has time for you.

How do I know that prayer will bring you closer to God? You can't say you know someone if you've never spent any time talking to him. The reverse side of the coin is that the more time you do spend talking to someone, the better you'll get to know him.

Perhaps you've heard the philosophy of Dwight L. Moody, one of the most famous evangelists this country has ever produced. It is said of Moody that

he would spend at least an hour in prayer every morning, except when he knew he was facing an exceptionally busy day. In that case, he would spend two hours in prayer. He wanted to be as sure as he could be that he was doing what God wanted him to do during the day—that he was handling every situation correctly.

I admit that it's not easy to cultivate that sort of an attitude. It's easy to let God get squeezed out of the day, especially if there are other 'more important' matters facing us. The truth is that there is nothing more important than developing a close relationship with our heavenly Father.

Furthermore, many of those who do take the time to pray on a daily basis never give much thought to what they're praying about. They never go very far beyond a perfunctory, "Bless me, Father." They don't spend the time to really open us and share their innermost thoughts with Him. Now make no mistake about it. God already knows all of your innermost thoughts the moments you think them, but Scripture makes it clear that He wants us to open our hearts up to him. This is for our benefit, because as we open ourselves up to Him, we get to know Him better. And, a funny thing about it is that as we open ourselves up to Him we get to know ourselves better, too.

In order to get to know God better through prayer, I make the following recommendations:

- ❑ Set aside time to spend in prayer every day. You may start out with five minutes, or you may start out with an hour. The important thing is to make prayer a daily habit, and spend

enough time that you are doing more than praying a "Father, bless me" prayer and going over your "wish list."

- ❑ Find a time of day for prayer that is best for you. Some people like to get out of bed and have a prayer time first thing in the morning, but others find themselves drifting back to dreamland so early in the morning. There is no single best time for prayer. God is always there and always ready to listen, so pick a time when you're most alert and best able to collect your thoughts.
- ❑ Prepare for your prayer time. Write down some areas of your life where you really need God's help. Perhaps there are some weaknesses where you know you need God's strength, some sore spots where you need God's strength, some sore spots where you need His guidance or healing, and even some victories and accomplishments you want to share with Him and thank Him for. Remember that prayer is not just asking God for things. It is simply talking to Him as you would talk to any other friend.
- ❑ If possible, find a place to pray where you will be free from distractions and interruptions. It should be a place where you are comfortable and which is conducive to a prayerful attitude.

Practising Meditation

Meditation is the second of the four things you can do to get closer to God. We have discussed this

previously, and I want to remind you that there is a substantial difference between Christian meditation and transcendental meditation. The primary difference is that Christian meditation is focused on God. Transcendental meditation calls on its adherents to empty their minds of all thoughts, whereas Christian meditation says that we should fill our minds with thoughts of God — His power, His mercy, His love, and His righteousness.

Many of the texts have to do with the importance of meditation.

You can't do much meditating in five minutes. The very word implies spending some time thinking about things. In this case it means thinking about the greatness of God and letting those thoughts feed your heart and soul until His greatness becomes very real to you.

Christian meditation has another connotation as well. Part of meditating is listening to what God is saying. This is also part of prayer, which is a conversation with God, but it's not much of a conversation if it's all going in one direction. In prayer and meditation we let God speak to us. Isn't it odd that many people spend more time talking to God and telling Him what they think they want than they do listening to Him to find out what they really want?

Now I can just hear someone saying, "Wait a minute! Do you actually expect God to speak to me?"

Well, probably not in an audible voice, although He might, but I do expect that, if you actually spend some time listening, He will give you insights into specific situations and clarity of mind as you confront

those situations. Remember, God often speaks in that small, quiet voice within. Oftentimes, that voice is in direct competition with the other voices and thoughts that are flitting around in a person's head. I believe that the more time you invest in meditation, the better you will be able to hear God and know His voice when He was something to say to you.

Reading the Bible

One of the primary ways God speaks to us today is through the Bible.

It is within the pages of this book that the nature of God is revealed to us. Here we read about the compassionate God who chose a downtrodden nation of slaves to become His people—the nation into which the Messiah would be born. We can read about how that same Jesus Christ was willing to die so that the rest of us might obtain eternal life. The Bible tells us the way God wants us to live, how He wants us to treat each other, and how He wants us to approach Him.

What kind of God do we have? First, He is a God of love, who cares deeply for every one of us—so deeply that He is willing to experience extreme pain in order to express His love and offer His grace. Second, He is a God of power, who can create, recreate and sustain—a God who has the power to create entire universes just by speaking.

He is a God who understands where you are and what you've been through, who has a plan for your life and is willing to direct you as you seek the unfolding of that plan. That is the God whom you

need to have at the center of your life and that is the God who is revealed in the Bible.

When that God is at the center of your life, when you have discovered His will for you and are moving in that direction, then you will begin to find more peace, joy, happiness, and security.

Taking the time to read and meditate on Scriptures such as that one can't help but encourage you and bring you closer to God.

I remember reading, a few years ago, about a group of Christian women who were hiking in the mountains when a flash flood hit their area. Rivers in the area roared over their banks. Roads and bridges were washed away. The hikers were stranded for several days while a search party looked for them. Finally, they were rescued—wet and cold, but otherwise unharmed.

When someone asked one of the hikers if she had been frightened during her ordeal, she replied that she would have been, except that she had memorised many of God's promises in the Bible. When things were at their worst and fear was beginning to take over, she would think about all of the wonderful things He has promised to those who love Him. She would share those Scriptures with the other women in her party, and they would all find comfort in the fact that God was with them, that He was looking our for them.

This woman said she and her friends knew that even if help didn't come, they were in God's hands, and that His will for them was for their ultimate benefit. Even if they had to die there on that mountain,

they knew through the Scriptures that God was with them, and that their ultimate fate was eternal life with Him in heaven!

That's the sort of strength and hope that comes from spending time reading and meditating on God's Word, letting its roots sink down into your heart.

Jesus talked about the importance of having good things in your heart when He said:

> The good man brings good things out of the good stored up in him, and the evil man brings evil things out of the evil stored up in him.

When you have the Word of God stored in your heart, you can't help but bring forth good things — both for your own life and for the lives of others. Read the Book He gave us and you will get to know God better. As you get to know Him better, you will be happier, stronger, and more able to live the kind of life He wants you to live.

The Importance of Fellowship

The fourth way in which you can get closer to God is through spending time with others who are also striving to be closer to Him. We've discussed this in some detail in chapter two, but I'll just remind you here that God designed us so that we need other people. There is always strength in numbers, whether you're talking about strands of thread joined together to make a rope or lives of people who are striving to be all that God wants them to be.

I believe that we all need to be part of larger group of people who share our goals and ideals, and

I also believe that it's important to have one other person to whom you can be especially close. Whenever you're trying to do something that is difficult for you, you'll find the going easier if you have a partner.

Are you trying to get in shape? Chances are very good that you'll do better if you have a friend who has the same goal, who can rejoice with you in your victories, console you in your defeats, and encourage you to hang on when you feel yourself giving in to temptation. That's why Alcoholics Anonymous works with meetings and sponsors. That's why churches with small groups are growing.

Want to give up smoking? The same is true there. Or drinking? It works in the negative areas and in the positive areas, too. Whatever you're trying to do with your life, it helps to have a "significant other" who can lend you a helping hand.

Do you have a significant other? That's someone you can call and with whom you can share your deepest hurt, frustrations, failures, joys, and hopes. My significant other is my wife, Donna. We always share our deepest thoughts with each other. Everyone needs someone like that. If you don't already have someone you can trust — with whom you can relax and share your innermost thoughts — you need now to invest some effort in finding that person. How good it is to have someone you can call any time of the day or night, who will listen, understand, and encourage you!

As you go through the days, there will be times of fear, indecision, and temptation. To be spiritually

mature doesn't mean that you will never experience fear, that you'll never be uncertain about what to do, or that you'll never yield to temptation. Spiritual maturity means that you'll keep pressing on in spite of the times when you are afraid. It means that you will seek God's will when the decision is difficult and know that He will be with you and sustain you even if the decision you make appears to be wrong. Spiritual maturity means that with God's help you will resist temptation, but it is also the assurance that He will not turn His back on you if you should stumble.

When you run into those moments of fear, indecision, or temptation, you need to stop and pray — anytime, anywhere — and ask God to help you deal with them. Then, if possible, the next thing to do is to call your significant other — your support person — who will listen and understand what you're going through.

Moving Through the Day

A group called Friends in Recovery has published an excellent little book called *The Twelve Steps for Christians*[1]. The authors present some guidelines for praying and meditating as you move through the day. I think those guidelines are well worth discussing here.

As the Day Begins

The authors suggest that at the beginning of each day you review your plans and ask God for direction in your thoughts and actions. Ask Him to keep you free from self-pity, dishonesty, and selfishness. Ask Him to provide the guidance you'll need to take care of

any problems that might arise during the day. Then, ask Him for freedom from self-will — specifically to avoid praying for your own selfish desires.

During the Day

As moments of need come to you, ask God for continual inspiration and guidance. It is also important at these times that you reflect back to step three, which was "I will turn my life over to God." Remember that we discussed the fact that this is not a "once-for-all-time" decision, but something that must be done again and again on an almost daily basis. This includes turning every difficult situation over to Him. Remember, even the situations that look impossibly difficult to you, God can handle with ease.

The authors of *The Twelve Steps for Christians* suggest that as you face these difficult moments, you stop, relax, and breathe deeply several times. This is an excellent idea because it allows you to concentrate on the fact that the battle is not yours, but the Lord's, and that He is more than up to the challenge.

Finally, if it is possible, call a support person — your significant other — and enlist his or her help in whatever struggles you're facing.

At the End of the Day

It's an excellent idea to take some time every evening to go back over the events of the day.

- Reflect on step ten: "*I will continue to take personal inventory of my life on a regular basis and promptly admit it when I do something wrong or lapse back into old behaviour patterns.*" With that in mind, take a personal inventory of your day and ask

God for His guidance and help in taking any corrective actions that might be necessary.

- Ask God for knowledge of His will for you.
- Ask God's forgiveness where needed. Keep in mind, however, that this review of your day is not intended to cause you excessive worry or remorse — either over what you did that you shouldn't have, or what you didn't do that you should have.
- Thank God for His guidance and blessings during the day.

I know I've said it before but I have to say it again — do not get down on yourself if you find yourself stumbling from time to time. We are all human and we all experience failure. You may not have arrived at where you want to be, but you are headed in the right direction — in fact you have come a very long way in the right direction — and that is what's important. Some of you have had victories over some very heavy issues here — promiscuity; addiction to drugs, alcohol, or tobacco; co-dependency; and others — so don't berate yourself because of your failures. Acknowledge them, yes. Strive to do better, absolutely. But encourage yourself, as well, by taking a long look at your successes and thanking God for His help in achieving them.

We have now gone through eleven steps. If you have been serious about following them as you've progressed through this book, I know that you have experienced a drastic change in your life. Do you feel good about where you are right now compared to where you were when we started this journey?

You have a right to feel good about yourself. It's okay to reach around and pat yourself on the back and say, "Congratulations! You're really doing a great job!"

So go ahead and do that. Then we'll move on to the twelfth and final step.

12
Spread the News

Since you have found some truth that has changed your life, you probably want to share it with as many people as possible. That's what the twelfth and final step is all about.

I will seek to carry to others the glorious
message of the possibility of a
spiritual awakening.

When I hear the term 'spiritual awakening,' I always wonder what people have in mind. Because I am a minister, people often tell me about some sort of spiritual awakening. I'm sure they think I'm going to be impressed by what has happened to them — and sometimes I am impressed — but it's also true that I have heard some very strange stories presented in the guise of spiritual awakenings.

Some people seem to think that a spiritual awakening has to involve visions or voices or strange lights shining down from heaven. These things may take place once in awhile, but the sort of spiritual awakening we're talking about here is one that is very much down to earth. It involves a rock solid understanding of life that begins with the realisation that we live our lives as an expression of God's will. That relates to the very first step we took — remembering that we are powerless in ourselves.

With the realisation that we are powerless must come the recognition that God is all-powerful, that, He is in control, and because of that our lives have meaning, purpose, and a foundation on which we can build the rest of our lives.

That is the beginning of a spiritual awakening that can revolutionise and revitalise the human spirit. A spiritual awakening causes us to realise that it doesn't matter what we used to be or causes us to realise that it doesn't matter what we used to be or how we used to live. Things are going to be different from now on, thanks to our recognition of the power of God in our lives.

Has your journey through the twelve steps helped to bring about a spiritual awakening in your life? Then you need to share that news with others—for at least two reasons.

One, it will help to solidify the changes that have taken place in your life. Telling other people about your spiritual awakening can't help but make it seem even more real to you and help to drive home the point that you no longer have to live the way you used to live.

Two, sharing the good news with others may help to rescue them from lives of confusion and desperation.

John C. remembers the day he invited his friend Rosie to go to an AA Meeting. Rosie seemed to be a hopeless drunk. He even had John stop on the way to the meeting so he could buy a beer. But John wouldn't give up because he wanted Rosie to experience what he himself had experienced—and sure enough, that's exactly what happened. AA and its Twelve-Step program changed Rosie's life, too.

This was a man who had never held a steady job but had occasionally earned money as a gardener. He was a man whose little children were always ill-fed and ragged.

God's power, working through a Twelve-Step program, helped Rosie stay sober for the last thirty-five years of life. He was able to get a good job with the parks department in his town, and by the time he died he was the head of maintenance for that department. Spurred on by his role modelling, his children have all developed into good, upstanding, productive leaders of their community.

That's the sort of thing that happens when you share the news!

The Importance of the Foundation

Sharing the good news with others will strengthen your foundation while encouraging others to experience the same spiritual awakening. If you want to build a good life you have to have a good foundation, and that foundation begins with a spiritual awakening, the realisation that your own weakness doesn't matter because God can be strong for you.

Over the years, my father and I have worked together on a couple of different building projects. When I was thirteen, we started building a cabin near Big Bear Lake—high up in the San Bernardino Mountains. I remember the first time I saw the lot my dad had bought. It was listed on the tax rolls in the city of Big Bear as 'unbuildable', but he bought it because he thought he *could* build there. I agreed with the city. I thought there was no way in the world we were going to be able to build anything on that land, and my father had invested his inheritance in it.

Inspite of my lack of faith, we built a cabin on the 'unbuildable lot,' and it all started with a strong, deep foundation. The cabin is still in excellent condition today, even after the 6.8 earthquake of 1992! About fifteen years ago my dad gave it to the Crystal Cathedral, and today the staff members use it as a place of retreat. It really is a beautiful place, in spite of my first misgivings.

I recall another building project that didn't fare as well. This time, my dad decided to build a horse corral. Somebody had given my sister Carol a horse, and she immediately discovered that she loved horseback riding. I was in my early twenties at the time, and my dad called and asked if I could come out and help him with a project. I didn't know until I got there that the project was a corral for my sister's horse.

When he told me what he wanted to do, I said, "Okay. Where are the plans?"

"I don't have any," came his reply.

"No plans?"

"No. Here grab this." He handed me a sheet of plywood, grabbed a couple of two-by-fours, and started nailing them to the plywood.

Well, that's how we started, and we wound up with a kind of strange-looking contraption that wasn't like any horse corral I've ever seen before or since. It stood there for a few years — before a strong wind came along one day and collapsed the entire thing. Fortunately, the horse wasn't there when it fell down.

The major difference between those two buildings was that one had a solid foundation, but the other had no foundation at all. The one with the foundation is still standing tall and proud, but the one without a foundation has long since disappeared from the scene.

The implication is obvious: If you are trying to build your life without any real foundation, you are going to wind up with nothing more than a heap of rubble. If you are building on a solid foundation, pouring a cement base and attaching it to solid rock, it could be leaning on the side of a hill, but it could last forever.

God Is Blessing You Now

A life that is built on a spiritual foundation is lived with the attitude that wherever I go, whatever I am doing, 'God is blessing me now.' It's true, you know. God is blessing you—right now!

After I had taught this on *The Hour of Power* broadcast I received a letter from a woman in Arizona who said she was writing to thank me for my message. She told me that it had changed her life, and that she had decided that whatever she did from then on, she would do it with the attitude that God was blessing her now.

She went on to stare how she had taken a trip in her motor home to visit relatives in Arizona. The trip didn't start off too well and had a good chance of turning into a complete disaster. She held onto the idea that God was blessing her right then, and one by one all of those potential disasters turned into beautiful blessings. Everywhere she turned, she said, she saw the hand of God directly blessing her.

All I can say to that is, 'Wow!' It's true, and it works. The person who has had a spiritual awakening will know that the hand of God is in whatever is going on in his life, and he will have the assurance that God wants only the best for him. You can count on that without reservation because it is absolutely true!

One Sunday morning not too long ago, as I came into our sanctuary, one of the members of our church stopped me and said, 'You know, Robert, God is really blessing me today!'

When I asked him how, he started off by telling me that he'd had a flat tire on his motorcycle on the way to church. Now, that didn't sound like much of a blessing to me. But then he related how, when he pulled off to the side of the road, another person stopped to help him. He and the man who stopped had an immediate rapport and became friends. He figured that a flat tire was a very small inconvenience when measured alongside the lasting value of a new friendship—and he was blessed by the encouragement that came from knowing that there are people who are ready and willing to help in times of trouble.

What is going on in your life right now? It may not be immediately pleasant, but you have to understand that God is still blessing you. Does that mean He caused you to be sick, brought about the breakup of your marriage, or caused you to be laid off from your job? No, of course not. But it does not mean that even in the midst of any terrible thing that might be happening to you, God can bless you. If you will look for His hand in your affairs, you will see His blessings in your life.

Remember, all things work together for the good of those who love God. That means that God can turn even the most trying situations to your advantage—whether we're talking about something as minor as a flat tire or something as major as the loss of a job.

A spiritual awakening begins with a foundation built on the realisation that God is in control of your life. It is furthered by the realisation that God is blessing you now, and it moves on into the future, redirecting your aims and goals toward things that are of real and lasting value. We are no longer held captive by our basic instincts and needs but free to be other-directed and God-directed.

For most of us, this awakening doesn't happen immediately, with a drumroll or a blinding flash. Instead, it happens gradually, over time. Then one day we look at our lives and see that we have a different attitude than we used to have. We think about things in a different way. Those walls that used to surround us have begun to crumble, and we can reach out in love to those around us.

These are some of the ways that God blesses. Take a good and honest look at your life, and I'm sure you'll see many other areas of His blessing as well.

Even a difficult past is part of God's blessing today. How can that be? Because all that has happened to you in the past—whatever it may have been, no matter how painful—has brought you to where you are today. When you look at your past you may see a life that was totally without direction or foundation, but it was those difficult times as much as anything else that brought you to God—so even the bad times ultimately turned out to be for your benefit.

To better explain what I'm talking about, let me tell you about my children, Christina and Anthony.

Not long ago, Christina was in kindergarten and that meant she was learning all of her letters and starting to write sentences. This opened up a whole new world for her, and she just loved to learn how to spell new words. She'd colour a picture and then want to write down what colour she used. So she'd ask, 'Dad, how do you spell black?' or 'Mom, how do you spell red?' Then she'd show us what she'd done. 'See, Mummy, this is red,' and so on.

Her brother, Anthony, watched her and, like little brothers everywhere, he wanted to be able to do the same things his big sister was doing. He'd try. 'Daddy, how do you spell black?'

'It starts with a B?'

Then he'd say, 'What's a B?'

Because he hadn't been to school, he didn't have any idea how to form the various letters of the alphabet. I could stand there all day telling him how to spell things, but it wouldn't do him a bit of good. Not until he learned how to distinguish an A from a B or a C or any other letter, would he be able to put those letters together and form words with them.

In the same way, if we try to live our lives totally removed from our past, it's like saying, 'How do you spell *red*?' God tells us, but we don't understand what He's talking about.

In other words, all of our past experiences, if they have benefited us in no other way, have at least taught us something about ourselves and the world in which we live.

All the turmoil that you may have had in your childhood, all the disappointments you may have experienced in your relationships with others, all that has happened in your life has made you the person you are and has brought you to the place where you are today. This gives you the right to talk to others who are where you were. You can share with them how you have progressed through the Twelve Steps and invite them to do the same and begin this journey of spiritual awakening.

I Was Blind, But Now....

The ninth chapter of John contains a beautiful example of a man who followed the principle found in this twelfth step. It is in the story of an encounter between the Lord and a man who was born blind. When a person is born blind, it is unlikely that he is ever going to receive his sight. Sometimes when an older person is blinded by cataracts, corrective surgery will restore sight, but when a child is born blind there is usually nothing that anyone can do about it.

If you have observed someone who has undergone surgery for cataracts—who can see after being nearly blind—you know what a wonderful thing that is. Getting your sight back after losing it is a fantastic miracle.

Imagine what it was like for the man who was born blind. He had never seen anything; a sunset, the face of a friend, his own face in a mirror. He had no idea that the world was full of beautiful colours.

Then he comes in contact with Jesus, the one who created colour, and his eyes are opened. For the first time in his life, he really begins to understand and appreciate the beauty of this world.

When Jesus' disciples first encountered the blind man, they wanted to know who had sinned and thereby caused the man to be born blind—the man himself or his parents. It's an odd thought. Would God punish an innocent baby for something his parents has done? No. Physical problems of this nature are not the result of any sort of disobedience to God, and Jesus was quick to put the disciples straight. He answered the question this way: 'Neither this man nor his parents sinned… but this happened so that the work of God might be displayed in his life.' Modern psychology is finding that this sort of question isn't so farfetched. God doesn't punish a child because of the sins of his parents, but there are natural consequences to sinful behaviour, and these often impact children. God says that children and even grandchildren will feel the repercussions of a parent's or grandparent's sin. For example, children of an alcoholic will often become alcoholics themselves. There's a good probability that their children and their children's children will also become alcoholics. It is a sin that perpetuates itself. In the same way, a child who is abused by his parents is likely to become an adult who abuses his children.

The question 'Who sinned... this man or his parents?' haunts us even today. We see that wrong behaviour on the part of parents can have a profound and lasting effect on the lives of their children. Remember, for instance, what happened to my wife, Donna, who found refuge in drinking while she was still in junior high school. She had learned that this was a way of handling things from what she observed in her parents.

The good news is that a cycle of behaviour such as this can be broken through following the Twelve Steps we have been discussing in this book—just as it was broken in Donna's life.

So too with the blind man. I'm sure that his was an eye-opening experience in more ways than one. No doubt there had been many times when this man, sitting alone in his darkened world, had wondered if God cared about him at all. Perhaps he had even wondered if God really even existed. But now there could be no doubt, either that God existed or that God cared about him—and cared deeply. Only God could have given him his sight. This man had a profound spiritual awakening.

Not everyone was happy about what happened. The Pharisees, the religious leaders of the day, were especially upset. They didn't like Jesus or the radical things He was saying, and they certainly weren't happy about His backing up His words with such a display of power.

The Pharisees asked this man who had opened his eyes, and they asked him in such a tone of voice that he knew very well that they were not happy about it. He told them that a man had put mud on his eyes and when he washed it off he could see. They weren't at all happy with this answer, and demanded to know who this man was.

This time, he answered them by saying that the man who did it was a prophet.

This answer indicates the progression of his spiritual awakening. At first he said that 'a man' opened his eyes. Then after he had thought about it a little bit more, he knew that the one who did this was, at the very least, a prophet.

As for the Pharisees, they still weren't satisfied, so they brought the man's parents in and asked them what had happened. Naturally, the parents were frightened by the Pharisees' threatening manner and said, 'He's old enough to tell you what happened. Ask him, not us'.

Isn't it interesting that the Pharisees completely overlooked the fact that something wonderful had happened to this fellow? They didn't care if the man could see. They only wanted to accuse Jesus.

As to the man's assertion that the one who had restored his sight was a prophet, the Pharisees contemptuously replied that this was far from the truth. In fact, they snorted, Jesus was a sinner. The blind man—or rather, the formerly blind man—replied, 'Whether he is a sinner or not I do not know. One thing I know; that though I was blind, now I see.' Certainly, he was being sarcastic with that answer because he knew for certain that no sinner could perform such a miracle.

And from that time on, you can be sure that this man spent as much time as possible telling others about the spiritual awakening that had been brought to him through his encounter with the Son of God. He told those who were blind—both physically and spiritually—that it was possible for them to see. He spoke from personal experience, and this compelled others to listen to him.

Are You Ready to Live?

Not too long ago my father told me an interesting story about the time Roman Catholic Bishop Fulton Sheen spoke at the Crystal Cathedral. I was no more than eight or nine years old at the time, so I don't remember the event that well, but my father recalls the momentous day.

Fulton Sheen was one of the most effective religious communicators of his time. His weekly television broadcast was the most popular program in the country. It was so popular, in fact, that it clobbered Milton Berle's comedy show in the ratings, with the result that Berle's program was cancelled.

To understand the magnitude of this achievement, just imagine how people would react if the Crystal Cathedral's Hour of Power knocked a popular show like *Roseanne* off the air.

And what did Bishop Sheen do to achieve such terrific ratings? He talked to people—that's all. Despite that simple format, his became the most popular show in America.

Because he was so popular, thousands of people came to hear him at the Crystal Cathedral. After the message, he and my father were able to get to their car only because a passage was roped off. Otherwise, they would have been mobbed. All along both sides of the ropes, people were reaching out in an attempt just to touch the bishop. It was as if the pope himself had come to town.

As Bishop Sheen was passing through this section on his way to his car, someone, handed him a note, which he folded and put into his pocket. Then, as he and my father were on their way to the restaurant where they were going to eat lunch, Bishop Sheen pulled that note out of his pocket, read it, and asked my father, 'Do you know where this trailer park is?'

My dad looked at the note and said, 'Yes, it's just a couple of miles from here.'

The bishop said, 'Do you think we could go there before we go to lunch?'

'Sure', my dad answered. 'We have plenty of time.'

So they drove to this little trailer park, and my father waited while Bishop Sheen went up to one of the trailers and knocked on the door. An elderly woman opened the door, and seemed surprised—flabbergasted, really—when she saw who had come to visit her. She opened the door and the bishop went in.

After a few moments, he came out, got back in the car and said, 'Now she's ready for living—in this life—but who most certainly wasn't ready to live in the next'. He was helping her get ready to do both.

That's what happens when you have a spiritual awakening. It gives you the strength and vision to live now, and it also prepares you for the life that lies beyond this one.

Were you blind, until God restored your sight?

Were you living in darkness, until God brought you into the light?

Were you struggling with fear and anger, until God restored you with his peace and joy?

If you have had such a spiritual awakening, you need to do your best to present others with the same opportunity. How can you do that?

- By letting others see the changes that, by the grace of God, have taken place in your life. The old saying is true: Actions do speak louder than words. The best way to show the way to spiritual renewal is to live in peace and happiness.
- By being open to opportunities to share with others the principles that are incorporated in this book. Do you know someone who's struggling in life right now? Perhaps you could give him a copy of this book or another book on the Twelve Steps. You could write a letter or make a phone call to tell someone how you have benefited from these steps.

- ❑ By giving of your time and energy to a group that offers support to people who are where you once were and who are trying to get their lives in order.
- ❑ By being ready, whenever an opportunity presents itself, to open your mouth and tell other people about your God and what He has done in your life.

The Journey Begins

We have come now, to the end of this book, but it's the beginning of the rest of your journey through life. I hope this book has given you strength and encouragement for that journey.

I know it's done that if you have applied these Twelve Steps to your life. If you have worked at living up to the principles embodied in these steps, then I feel confident that you have experienced a spiritual awakening because these Twelve Steps follow precepts that are backed up by the power of God. They are sound principles and they work.

As you continue your spiritual growth and problems unfold in your life, you will be able to work and rework these steps and continue to grow closer and closer to God. No price is too great to pay and no effort is too great to make for a life that is being lived in the will of God and is therefore peaceful, ordered, and joyful.

The Serenity Prayer

God, grant me the serenity
to accept the things I cannot change,
the courage to change the things I can,
and the wisdom to know the difference.
Living one day at a time,
enjoying one moment at a time;
accepting hardship as a pathway to peace;
taking, as Jesus did,
the sinful world as it is,
not as I would have it;
trusting that You will make all things right
if I surrender to your will;
so that I may be reasonably happy in this life
and supremely happy with you forever in the next.
Amen.

REINHOLD NIEBUHR

This is a special poem that I keep before me. These words have made a difference in my life. I am confident that they will do the same in yours.

Robert A. Schuller

The Twelve Steps of Alcoholics Anonymous

1. We admitted that we were powerless over alcohol—that our lives had become unmanageable.
2. Came to believe that a Power greater than ourselves could restore us to sanity.
3. Made a decision to turn our will and our lives over to the care and direction of God as we understood Him.
4. Made a searching and fearless moral inventory of ourselves.
5. Admitted to God, to ourselves, and to another human being the exact nature of our wrongs.
6. Were entirely ready to have God remove all these defects of character.
7. Humbly asked Him to remove our shortcomings.
8. Made a list of all persons we had harmed, and became willing to make amends to them all.
9. Made direct amends to such people wherever possible, except when to do so would injure them or others.
10. Continued to take personal inventory and when we were wrong promptly admitted it.

11. Sought through prayer and meditation to improve our conscious contact with God as we understood Him, praying only for knowledge of His will for us and the power to carry that out.
12. Having had a spiritual awakening as the result of these steps, we tried to carry this message to alcoholics, and to practise these principles in all our affairs.*

*The Twelve Steps reprinted and adapted with permission of Alcoholics Anonymous World Services, Inc. Permission to reprint and adapt the Twelve Steps does not mean that AA has reviewed or approved the content of this publication, nor that AA agrees with the views expressed herein. AA is a program of recovery from alcoholism. Use of the Twelve Steps in connection with programs and activities which are patterned after AA but which address other problems does not imply otherwise.

Endnotes

Chapter Two

1. J.B.Phillips, *Your God is Too Small* (New York; Macmillan, 1964).
2. Corrie ten Boom, *The Hiding Place* (London: Hodder & Stoughton, Christian Literature Crusade, 1971).

Chapter Three

1. John Bradshaw, *Homecoming: Reclaiming and Championing Your Inner Child* (New York: Bantam Books, 1990).

Chapter Four

1. John Calvin, *Institutes of the Christian religion*, ed. Fort L Battles (Grand Rapids: Eerdman's, 1986).

Chapter Seven

1. C.S. Lewis, *Mere Christianity* (New York: MacMillan, 1963).
2. *Big Book of AA* (New York: Alcoholics Anonymous World Service, Inc.) 76.

Chapter Nine

1. Robert Fulghum, *All I Really Needed to Know I Learned in Kindergarten* (New York: Villard Books, 1988)

Chapter Eleven

1. *The Twelve Steps for Christians* (San Diego: Recovery Publications, Inc., 1988), 111-12.

Chapter Twelve

1. *Big Book of AA* (New York: Alcoholics Anonymous World Service, Inc.), 196.

Also in Orient Paperbacks

Secrets of Success

Charles Newton

Rs. 60.00

When was the last time you tried to punch a hole in the sky?

Tests Pilots, punching into stratosphere, climbing to undreamt heights in jets and rocket planes, have a phrase they use to describe their work.

They call it 'punching holes in the sky.'

That is what we are meant to do with our lives, to climb beyond the humdrum, to reach beyond the preoccupation of daily existence. However, more often that not, when it comes to living, we settle for the mediocre. The sky is too high to think of. It is the impossible that stops us. But nonetheless it is the challenge of the impossible that gets life out of its rut and onto a highway that leads us to our goal.

Think big, work hard and have the courage to dream.

Remember, if you don't care for your dreams, who will.

Whatever your personal goals, this book will help you become the person you have always wanted to be.